The TACO CLEANSE

THE TORTILLA-BASED DIET PROVEN TO
CHANGE YOUR LIFE

WES ALLISON ★ STEPHANIE BOGDANICH ★ MOLLY R. FRISINGER ★ JESSICA MORRIS

THE EXPERIMENT

NEW YORK

THE TACO CLEANSE: *The Tortilla-Based Diet Proven to Change Your Life*

Copyright © 2015 Wes Allison, Stephanie Bogdanich, Molly R. Frisinger, and Jessica Morris
Photographs copyright © 2015 Stephanie Bogdanich
Foreword © 2015 Laura Beck

First self-published in different form as a zine in the United States in 2013.

The Experiment, LLC
220 East 23rd Street, Suite 301
New York, NY 10010-4674
www.theexperimentpublishing.com

This book contains the opinions and ideas of its authors, plus large quantities of total BS. Although the recipes are intended to be accurate and tasty, all other content is solely intended to be hilarious. The authors and publisher are not engaged in rendering actual medical, health, or any other kind of personal professional services in the book. The authors and publisher specifically disclaim all responsibility for any liability, loss, or risk—including but not limited to roof-of-mouth burns, acquired phobia of other cleanses, and laughter-induced cramping—that is incurred as a consequence, directly or indirectly, of the use and application of any of the contents of this book. Oh, and no—plants don't crave electrolytes.

The Experiment's books are available at special discounts when purchased in bulk for premiums and sales promotions as well as for fund-raising or educational use. For details, contact us at info@theexperimentpublishing.com.

Library of Congress Cataloging-in-Publication Data

Allison, Wes.
  The taco cleanse : the tortilla-based diet proven to change your life /
Wes Allison, Stephanie Bogdanich, Molly R. Frisinger, and Jessica Morris.
     pages cm
  Includes index.
  ISBN 978-1-61519-272-4 (pbk.) -- ISBN 978-1-61519-273-1 (ebook)
1. Stuffed foods (Cooking) 2. Tortillas. 3. Vegan cooking. 4.
Reducing diets--Humor. 5. Cookbooks--Humor I. Bogdanich, Stephanie. II.
Frisinger, Molly R. III. Morris, Jessica (Cook) IV. Title.
  TX836.A45 2015
  641.8--dc23
                          2015015996

ISBN 978-1-61519-272-4
Ebook ISBN 978-1-61519-273-1

Book design by Sarah Smith
Cover photograph by Stephanie Bogdanich
Yoga, Salutations, and Mudras illustrations by Amey Mathews
Additional illustrations on pages 7, 12, 188, 191-193, and 205 by Jonas Madden-Connor; pages 20, 46, and 203 by Sarah Smith; viii and xiv by Wes Allison

Manufactured in Canada
Distributed by Workman Publishing Company, Inc.
Distributed simultaneously in Canada by Thomas Allen & Son Ltd.

First printing December 2015
10 9 8 7 6 5 4 3 2

Contents

THE BUILDING BLOCKS OF A TACO-BASED DIET 33

Condiments 113

Artist Tacos 137

Supplements 172

Foreword

Cleanses are the fucking worst. They're socially acceptable starvation disguised as health, and that is the fucking worst. Used largely as a tool to make women feel guilt about consuming real food and repent their eating "sins," they demand you choke down lemon juice swirled with cayenne pepper and your tears so that you can lose those last five pounds. Screw those last five pounds; your body clearly wants the extra chub if the only way to get rid of it is drinking juice made of lawn clippings, hot sauce, and your own choked-down vomit.

However, I must qualify this ranking, as not all cleanses are bad. One cleanse rises above the rest and makes you feel amazing in the four ways that matter most—as enumerated in Usher's "Love in This Club"—sexually, mentally, physically, and emotionally. That's right. I'm talking about the one and only Taco Cleanse. The empowering, guilt-free, and soul-satisfying journey you're about to take your body and mind through will be not only supremely delicious (as tacos are involved) but also life-changing.

Obviously, it makes sense that the stone-cold visionaries from the Austin vegan scene birthed this magnificent beast—I've never seen a group so committed to and guided by a taco philosophy. Let them hold your hand/garnish your taco (I meant that sexually) through your journey with recipes, crosswords, flowcharts, illustrations,

PowerPoint presentations, and voodoo. They'll lead you from your first taco shopping list all the way to cleanse graduation day—you'll walk away with an actual diploma that proves to the world that you are a taco-loving lunatic not to be messed with.

Taco speed, my little tacos.

Signed,
Laura Beck, *Vegansaurus*
Los Angeles, CA

Preface

Over the years I have changed my diet more times than I can count. Since childhood, really, I was on a quest to find what worked best for me. When I moved to Austin over ten years ago I started supplementing my diet with tacos, particularly breakfast tacos: the most important taco of the day. I wasn't seeing the results I was looking for. Sure, I would eat tacos most days, but then sometimes for dinner I would screw up by eating a burger or some soup. I had no self-control and I could hardly look at myself in the mirror anymore. It was also during this time I noticed a rash of physical symptoms. Sometimes I would feel really tired, especially in the morning when my alarm went off. Other times, I couldn't fall asleep at night. I knew this wasn't right! My body was trying to tell me something. Along with these issues I was filled with occasional bouts of melancholy and depression. I would ask myself, "Where is my life even going?"

Who knows how long I could have gone on this way? But lucky for me, and for you, I met up with a team of taco scientists prepared to nurture my fledgling taco habit and also give me the community of support that I needed to follow through on what came to be known as the Taco Cleanse. Together we forged a new path of wellness and self-discovery.

Having a community to support and help you along the way is one of the most important aspects of the Taco Cleanse. During the cleanse I found myself texting my fellow taco scientists, asking where to get late-night tacos or how to deal with social situations. Commit to cleansing with your friends, family, or coworkers, or follow along with the online taco cleansing community by using the hashtag #tacocleanse on Twitter, Instagram, and Facebook.

Below, my fellow taco scientists share their own journeys to taco enlightenment.

Stephanie Bogdanich

I knew relocating to Austin would be a much-needed shift in lifestyle. A decade of living in the ceaseless buzz of central Houston had taken its toll on my well-being. Overstimulation had caused a simmering anxiety below the surface, threatening to boil over into full-blown panic. This had become the new normal.

I began hearing tales of a city only hours away where verdant paths and icy creeks were woven into the fabric of the concrete landscape. A city where enlightened yogis and gutter punks walked hand in hand. A city where pedestrians traveled without restriction and commuters propelled themselves on fantastic vehicles. A city with bountiful feasts for every obscure dietary restriction. A city where festivals extended into perpetuity. Certainly, I thought, this utopia could not be real. I needed to confirm these rumors for myself.

Shortly after moving to the south side of Austin, I found that the stories were all true. My tension was releasing into the cosmos and my vitality was rapidly regenerating. It seemed that many others among the local townsfolk were also operating at a higher octave. Being scientifically minded, I needed to suss out the source of these benefits.

Months passed without any significant discoveries. There were too many variables. My first insight arrived when two friends visited for the weekend. In less than forty-eight hours, their complexions glowed and their irises clarified. Their vibrations were not only heightened but sustained. They were unwitting participants in my experiment. Their only lifestyle deviation was dietary. Since arriving in Austin, their sole source of sustenance had been tacos. We were on the verge of a breakthrough.

With three other taco scientists, I decided to subject myself to a monthlong trial. We vowed to eat nothing but tacos for every meal and report the results. During the experiment, the benefits were undeniable. We decided to dedicate our lives to educating others about the Taco Cleanse.

Maybe tacos are a weekly staple for you as they once were for me, or maybe you have never eaten a taco. Whatever your background, I invite you to join us on our taco journey.

Wes Allison

A s a kid, I dabbled in tacos. Growing up in Dallas–Fort Worth, they were just a part of life. Sunday mornings we'd gather at Casa Jose with family and friends for brunch. I would scan the menu every time, even though I knew I would eventually order two egg-and-chorizo tacos. As I got older, I transitioned to *migas* tacos, like the adults always ordered. Twenty years later, I can still recite everyone's taco orders.

And then I went off to college in the Northeast and quickly realized that not everyone ate tacos. It was shocking. I couldn't find good tortillas or salsa. For four years, I lived as if I were two people: one who studied foreign languages and tried to figure out how to buy a winter coat and another who made migas tacos with tomatoes and jalapeños straight from the garden.

Eventually, I moved back to Texas. My first night in Austin we went out for chips and salsa. I was home.

So when Stephanie suggested we go on a Taco Cleanse, I thought I knew what I was signing up for. I knew what it was like to go without tacos and what it was like to binge on tacos, trying to make up for misguided eating of ramen, pizza, and frozen burritos. I thought there was nothing left for me to learn.

I was so wrong.

You see, I'd been battling several health issues. I constantly found strands of my hair in the shower or on my pillow. Like many of the women in my family, I found myself hungry in the middle of the afternoon and in the evenings. And I wasn't even sure if a child would be in my future. Before starting the Taco Cleanse, I had spent two years working with health professionals with what seemed like little progress.

Two weeks into a taco-based diet, my doctor told me, "You're doing everything right." It's no surprise that as I write this, my beautiful son is cooing by my side. I owe it all to the Taco Cleanse.

No one should have to sacrifice their health because they lack access to good taco-based foodstuffs. Many of these recipes are designed to be made with simple ingredients available from your neighborhood grocery store. There's no excuse for continuing on your current diet when delicious tacos are this easy. Wishing you health!

Molly R. Frisinger

I can't remember my first taco. I would have been pretty young, and it would have had a crunchy shell with the standard meat, cheese, lettuce, and tomato. We would go to a little local Tex-Mex restaurant and I'd order cheese enchiladas, while my sister got tacos. She loved salsa but hated guacamole. I would trade her an enchilada for a taco and take all of her guacamole. I definitely came out ahead.

At home, we'd lay out taco fillings on the counter, so everyone could build their own. It was an easy, cheap, fun meal. When I went vegetarian at thirteen, I just swapped the taco meat for refried beans. In college, I started hanging out with vegans and decided that I could make the transition, too, as long as there were taco options. I was only a novice cook, and finding vegan substitutes for taco meat and cheese in the late 1990s wasn't easy. My refried bean and guacamole tacos weren't terrible, but they weren't terribly exciting, either.

I worked for Whole Foods Market in Dallas about the time when companies decided to try their hand at vegan meat and dairy analogs, and I got to sample them all. Creating vegan tacos became so much easier. Add some browned veggie taco meat, shredded plastic-tasting vegan cheese, chopped tomato, and a dollop of vegan sour cream to a tortilla, and taco night was done.

Flash forward a couple of decades, and this is still how I cook. I am a convenience-food vegan, a junk-food vegan, a lazy vegan, a plant eater who rarely eats plants. Luckily, the age of vegan convenience foods is now. Vegan cheese has progressed beyond all belief to become delicious, meltable, flavorful, and widely available in dozens of varieties and brands. There are so many varieties of plant milk, it's hard to keep up. And veggie taco meat? Check any supermarket in the country and you'll surely find at least one brand.

How does a junk-food vegan end up becoming a taco scientist? Well, someone needed to highlight the convenience taco. The "I don't have time to cook" taco. The "I don't know how to cook" taco. That was right up my alley. I ate tacos with tater tots inside, tacos with chopped-up pizza inside, even tacos with a microwave burrito inside! It was glorious. I felt my levels increasing. My entire life ignited with passion. I realized that tacos are what you make them, and all tacos are created equal. The Taco Cleanse gave me a reason to believe—and it can do the same for you, whether you love to cook or hate it. Let's start today!

Jessica Morris

Ceci n'est pas une taco

IS THE TACO CLEANSE RIGHT FOR YOU?

T here are many reasons people consider embarking on a cleanse. Some feel that their vibrations could be higher. Others feel that their glow is in need of recharging. A select few wish to push their vitality to the next summit. Regardless of the reason, your life will change for the better when you adopt a new mind-set, realign your diet, and consume large quantities of tacos.

Please take a moment to answer this questionnaire and discover if you can benefit from a Taco Cleanse:

→ **Do you experience recurring feelings of hunger on a daily basis?**

→ **Do you frequently lack access to eating utensils such as forks or chopsticks?**

→ **Do you consider tortillas to function as edible napkins?**

→ **Do you enjoy attention from peers based on dietary restrictions?**

→ **Do you experience a range of emotions?**

→ **Do you tilt your head when inserting food into your mouth?**

→ **Do you use medical websites to self-diagnose your symptoms?**

Answering yes to any of these questions may indicate that a Taco Cleanse is right for you.

Your taste buds have an innate wisdom separate from the conscious mind. Perform this simple test and find out what your tongue already knows: Drink a jar of pure unadulterated salsa. If you react with hesitation or discomfort, your body needs help calibrating its disposition. Some of the most detuned bodyminds will perceive a warming sensation or produce light perspiration. If this happens to you, we recommend a drastic shift to a taco-compliant diet.

In this book, we open the doorway to a new perspective on cleansing. We hope you walk through and experience taco-based vitality forever. *Namaste*.

THE HOWS AND WHYS OF THE TACO CLEANSE

In the current era of superfoods and detox diets, many trends have failed to deliver on their promises. Goji, açai, chia, grapefruit, and countless others have gained momentary prominence only to return to obscurity. However, a small tribe of herbivorous Austinites has benefited from a previously unresearched native Texan delicacy . . . the taco. With recent scientific confirmation of the taco's mystical properties, we are able to share our results with the public. The following is our detailed research.

TACO CLEANSE

1 DAY	•At the mild level your mood will improve
3 DAYS	•At the medium level you will notice more energy
1 WEEK	•Hot level will lead to a better outlook on life
1 MONTH	•Your entire life will IGNITE with passion

MILD
MEDIUM
HOT
FUEGO

The plan is actually quite simple. All of your meals must contain tacos. A short Mild cleanse can last for just one day. A Medium cleanse lasts three days. A Hot cleanse will last an entire week. But if you want to go full-on Fuego, it's all tacos every day for a month. It's up to you whether you want to start out with a Mild cleanse before working your way up to Fuego or jump straight into the deep end with a full month of tacos. As one would expect, the benefits of a high-taco diet become especially apparent as one approaches Fuego level.

Surprising to the taco scientists, the benefits of taco consumption depend on more than just how many tacos you eat; they vary based on time of day as well as tortilla type. A taco consumed within three hours of waking, colloquially called a "breakfast taco," has been anecdotally proven to erase the ill effects of the previous night's toxic indulgences.

TODAY I AM SMART ENOUGH TO CHOOSE A TACO-BASED LIFESTYLE.

A midday taco frequently results in more positive physical effects: increased glow and perspiration in the face and forehead, a sensual aura of cumin and garlic that's enticing to humans of all genders and sexual preferences, as well as a light and uplifting sensation in the root chakra.

The spicy taco consumed prior to sleep stimulates the nocturnal imagination and has been used by taco spiritualists to induce prophetic dreams. In particular, the thermal side effects of evening bean digestion have long been known to help regulate the body temperatures of primitive campers on frigid Texas winter nights.

Now, we want to be clear that supplementing—that is, drinking beverages that traditionally accompany tacos—is acceptable as long as you are getting all of your tacos in. Margaritas should be added on an as-needed basis for the top levels of the cleanse, but at Fuego you should be adding them at least a couple of times a week, working up to every day.

WHAT IS A TACO?

In the initial days of the cleanse, there was a lot of debate about what counted as a taco. Obviously breakfast tacos and traditional fillings like *carnitas*, beans, and potatoes counted. We even felt comfortable with the idea of a pad thai-co or a veggie burger taco. After all, it's pretty common to see Korean or Vietnamese tacos these days, so adding other cuisines into the mix didn't flummox us. It was when we left the realm of the traditional tortilla that we felt some uncertainty.

All four scientists had sampled the vegan Dutch taco at the Flavour Spot in Portland: a waffle wrapped around sausage with maple spread. None of us questioned its validity as a taco. But when one scientist wrapped a pancake around some sausage, it just felt wrong. What was the difference between that and a sandwich? What makes a taco different from a burrito or a wrap? What about falafel, Ethiopian *injera*, Indian *dosa*, Vietnamese *banh xeo*, or Chinese *moo shu*? And what about the taco salad?

> "Every taco has beauty, but not everyone can see it."
> —CONFUCIUS

That led us to a few rules. First of all, a burrito is never, ever a taco. Never. Anything with more than one fold falls into the wrap/burrito realm. And the tortilla or tortilla-like object shouldn't be bready, like pancakes, pita, or pizza. Waffles fall outside these parameters, but we decided to grandfather them in. That Flavour Spot waffle taco just felt so right to us. We also decided that using leaves like collard greens or romaine lettuce was fine, so long as we stuck with just one fold. And taco salad, while not actually a taco, makes a great transition food in the days just before and after cleansing.

Further testing showed that size is important. A taco shouldn't be too large. You should be able to pick it up with one hand. Two hands, and you're approaching burrito status. And it must be portable. If it's too messy to wrap in foil and throw in your bag on the way to work, it probably isn't a taco.

The taco police probably will (and definitely have) called us out on our definition. We've been told that not only must a taco be in a tortilla, but that it has to be a corn tortilla. Or that the filling has to be meat. We think that's silly. Food isn't static or unchangeable. It's a flexible entity that changes depending on who, when, and where. People move to new locations where they can't find the ingredients they're used to or can't afford them. People have dietary restrictions that keep them from the traditional versions of the food they love (we're spilling some salsa on the ground for our brethren with celiac disease). And besides, we don't want to live in a sad world that doesn't acknowledge flour tortillas, Gobi Manchurian, tomatoes in Italian food, or avocado in sushi.

Once we adopted these five rules, we immediately experienced a breakthrough. Our skin glowed, our walks were jauntier, and Wes's beard grew at an alarming rate.

The Taco, Defined

1. A taco has only one fold.
2. Tortillas must be flat, not bready.
3. But waffles are the exception.
4. A taco must be handheld and portable.
5. A burrito is never, ever a taco.

HOW TO PREPARE FOR A TACO CLEANSE

When you first decide to go on the Taco Cleanse, you might think it will be a cakewalk, or even a tacowalk, if you will. Before the first few days of transmorphing to an all-taco diet, however, you will realize that some preparation is going to be in order. Even in our hometown of Austin, Texas, where tacos are plentiful, they still don't have total market penetration. You will quickly learn that it's important to bring your own tortillas for emergencies and to always have some quick premade taco ingredients ready to go in your

fridge. Setting yourself up for success will make it easier to contemplate not only where your next taco is coming from, but also what your last taco is doing for you. The Taco Cleanse definitely takes some planning, but once you feel the benefits, you'll find that it's worth it.

With that said, here is a list of some of the ways you can keep your refrigerator stocked, your pantry full, and your bodymind relaxed:

Refried beans Either canned or homemade (see page 82); keep these on hand always.

Rice Brown or white, instant or regular; a rice cooker may come in handy.

Tofu scramble Our Wake and Shake Scramble can be made ahead of time (see page 96) and kept refrigerated.

Flour and corn tortillas Homemade or store-bought; flour will keep for a while, but corn should be eaten within a day or frozen for later.

Potatoes Russet, purple, and the occasional sweet; feel free to sub in new (red) potatoes.

Mushrooms Button, portobello, and oyster mushrooms will go in these recipes.

Our recipes are authentically Austin, where tacos contain Korean barbecue, roasted cauliflower, tempeh, and beets, as well as the more usual Mexican fillings. These are the tacos we grew up eating, inspired by our favorite restaurants, vegan cuisine, Costa Rica, Jamaica, California, and sometimes even Mexico, where the taco was first created. They reflect our belief that everything tastes better folded into a tortilla. If you'd like to read more about the history of tacos we recommend *Planet Taco: A Global History of Mexican Food* by Jeffrey M. Pilcher.

Romaine lettuce It's crisp and easy to shred or chop, and can be used as a tortilla.

Cilantro Unless your taste buds are broken, this herb will go on everything.

Tomatoes canned or fresh, all varieties; grow them in your Taco Garden (page 202).

A variety of peppers Jalapeño, habanero, and poblano are the most used.

Tomatillos In store-bought salsa (Tomatillo Heaven) or fresh.

Tofu Use extra-firm or firm packed in water. Drain and press for some recipes.

Tempeh Fear not this fermented soy food; it's been around for centuries!

Vegan chicharrones If you can find these, you will be the hit of the party.

Soy Curls Essentially just pulverized soybeans, these flavor-neutral dried strips will transform into fajitas, BBQ, and more. Find them online or at your health food store.

Nutritional yeast Used by ancient vegetarians to make food taste cheesy, these yellow flakes melt into nacho sauce and can be sprinkled directly onto tacos.

Tortilla chips Most are corn-based and accidentally vegan. Use with salsa and to scoop up fillings that drop out of the end of your taco.

I DECIDE WHAT I EAT AND TODAY I CHOOSE TACOS.

CORN OR FLOUR?

If you've ever thought, "I could never eat tacos ALL day," our guess is that you haven't had a really great tortilla. They are the most critical element of the taco, both for enfolding the delicious components within and for creating a way to bring the taco from your plate to your mouth. They are also a vital element when it comes to the taste and positive psychic effects of the taco. You hear a lot that you can tell a good taco stand from a bad taco stand by its salsa, but we disagree. Fresh homemade tortillas are the hallmark of any great taco stand. And they aren't even hard to make.

Choose your tortilla based upon its contents. Usually if it's going to be more of a Tex-Mex taco, like fajitas, or a scramble-sausage-cheese breakfast taco, use a flour tortilla. If it's more Mexican-inspired, like al pastor, carnitas, or a breakfast taco of refried beans, nopales, and potatoes, then choose a corn tortilla.

But really, flour vs. corn isn't even the real issue. It's quality. There are competing theories on the elemental effects of corn vs. flour. Some of the taco scientists recommend corn and some recommend flour. But we all agree that a good, fresh tortilla of any kind is the best. Generally you want to either make tortillas yourself or go somewhere where they are still warm when you purchase them. If you're stuck with only inferior options, a bad flour tortilla tends to be better than a bad corn tortilla. Flour tortillas are just more forgiving than corn. However, even bad store-bought tortillas can be improved by a short (fifteen- to thirty-second) trip through the microwave or a quick warm-up in a dry sauté pan or cast-iron skillet.

ALL THAT I SEEK IS WITHIN A TORTILLA.

You really should make your own, though. At least once. It's much easier than you think. Similar to making pancakes, but with fewer ingredients and in less time. There are recipes in this book for traditional and nontraditional tortillas. Corn tortillas are easier to cook, so you might start there. Tortillas don't last long, which is why dishes like migas, *chilaquiles*, and nachos were invented: to use up tortillas past their prime. Store freshly made tortillas in the fridge for a few days or in the freezer, separated by pieces of wax or parchment paper, for several weeks.

We have directions for making tortillas with and without a tortilla press, but we highly recommend watching a video before making your own. We have a few on our website (tacocleanse.com), but a quick YouTube search will also bring up several good ones.

"He who eats tacos should look to it that he himself does not become a taco. And when you gaze long into the filling, the filling also gazes onto you."
—NIETZSCHE

WHAT KIND OF TACO-EATER ARE YOU?

Taco cleansing isn't always easy. But trust us, there's a perfect taco out there for you. With the guidance of this quiz, you'll be rocking the Taco Cleanse all month long.

1. WHAT IS YOUR PREFERRED TACO WRAP?

a. Corn tortilla

b. Flour tortilla

c. Ancho chile-lime tortilla

d. Collard green leaf

2. YOU'RE SCANNING THE MENU OF A NEW TACO RESTAURANT; WHAT DO YOU ORDER?

a. Bean and potato taco; why mess with perfection?

b. Bean, potato, soyrizo, and avocado, just like your (imaginary) mom used to make

c. Japanese-fusion seitan *tonkatsu* taco with ponzu sauce

d. Falafel in pita is a kind of taco, right?

3. WHAT'S THE IDEAL NUMBER OF FILLINGS IN A TACO?

a. Two

b. Three

c. As many as will fit

d. Anything goes!

4. CHANGE IS

a. absolutely terrible

b. best avoided if possible

c. the best thing ever!

d. fine by you

5. RECIPES ARE

a. unnecessary. Simple ingredients and simple techniques don't need to be written down.

b. helpful for getting your salsa just the way Mom (or Diana Kennedy) used to make

c. a great resource for new taco ideas. Puttanesca taco, anyone?

d. nice to have around. There are so many kinds of tacos, no one can know them all.

6. YOU FIND A BAG OF DRIED BLACK BEANS FAR BACK IN YOUR CABINET. WAY FAR BACK. WHO KNOWS HOW LONG THEY'VE BEEN THERE? WHAT DO YOU DO?

a. Freak the hell out. Within an hour, all expired food has been disposed of and your kitchen counters are gleaming.

b. Put them back.

c. Pull out the takeout menus. This is obviously not the right time for a home-cooked meal.

d. If I cook them long enough, they'll be fine. Now where's the cumin?

IF YOU PICKED MOSTLY:

A's —You're a TACO PURIST. Deep in your heart you know that tacos were created right the first time. Korean tacos, spaghetti tacos, and dessert tacos are just distractions from the perfection of the one true taco. Others might call you boring or stuck in your ways, but you know that there's no improving a still-warm-from-the-comal corn tortilla with a smattering of fresh ingredients. During the Taco Cleanse, you might be especially vulnerable to food cravings due to your rigid definition of a taco. Be kind to yourself and venture beyond the strictest sense of the taco on occasion.

B's —You're a TACO SENTIMENTALIST. When you bite into a taco, you remember all the tacos of your youth. You think about Abuelita rolling out tortilla dough and ingredients sizzling on the stovetop, even if the *abuela* in your memory is the one drawn on the logo of your favorite tortillas. You don't mind trying something new or nontraditional, but your heart sings for the comfort of the tacos of yore. For you, taco cleansing will be a return to your roots. Embrace your sentimentality by making your own tortillas and cooking your beans from scratch.

C's—You're a TACO ADVENTURIST. Is it new? unusual? cross-cultural? Then you've just got to have it folded over in the latest flatbread craze. Whether you're searching out the newest fusion taco or re-creating a certain fast-food chain's Dorito-flavored taco shells, you're always after the next big taco innovation. Your passion for the new and exciting will keep you engaged during the Taco Cleanse, but beware. Sometimes, a taco is just a taco.

D's—You're a TACO CONTORTIONIST. Is it served on an edible flat food that's folded just once? Then it's a taco! You won't let the rules of the taco purist keep you back from filling your gut with wonderful tacos. Your one rule for tacos? Be delicious. While your easygoing nature makes it a snap for you to stick to the Taco Cleanse, don't forget the true roots of the taco, or one day you might find yourself calling a burrito a taco. For shame!

"If you really want to make a friend, go to someone's house and eat with him. The people who give you their taco give you their heart."

—CESAR CHAVEZ

BUT I HATE COOKING!

If you're about to embark on your Taco Cleanse, but you feel less than proficient in the kitchen, you're not alone. Many people want to enjoy the benefits of a Taco Cleanse, but hate to cook. If you live in a taco-centric part of the world (such as Austin, Texas), you'll have no trouble finding tacos at pretty much every restaurant you go to. If you do find it difficult to find tacos in your town, never fear; there are plenty of taco convenience foods at your local grocery or health food store. Using these products and staples, such as extra-firm tofu and nutritional yeast (aka nooch!), you can create delicious tacos in minutes.

Some of our favorites include:

Tofutti Sour Supreme, Better Than Sour Cream Tofutti has been around forever. The company makes some excellent vegan products such as ice cream treats, cream cheese, and cheese slices. The Sour Supreme is still the best-tasting sour cream on the market today.

Wholly Guacamole You can usually find this premade guacamole in tubs or single-serving containers in the refrigerated section of your supermarket. It's especially convenient when you can't find a ripe avocado at the store and don't want to wait three days for guacamole.

Upton's Naturals Seitan Chorizo or Bacon The chorizo from Upton's is less oily than other brands and adds a nice kick to any taco. The bacon strips are sliced thin so you can fry them in a pan and watch them sizzle.

Soyrizo (El Burrito or Melissa's brands) These are fairly easy to find, even sold at some Walmarts. The Soyrizo comes in a plastic tube, and part of the fun is squeezing it onto your skillet. Check the package; some brands are gluten-free.

Lightlife Gimme Lean Sausage Open a tube of Gimme Lean if you want some easy breakfast sausage that you can make any size. It's sticky when raw, so you have to be careful, but you can roll it into little sausage balls or drop it into oil in random chunks.

Lightlife Smart Ground Mexican Style Lightlife also makes taco meat that you just brown in a pan for a few minutes. It's already flavored and spiced, so talk about easy.

Daiya Pepperjack Style Shreds Daiya is one of the companies propelling vegan cheese into the mainstream. Their Pepperjack Style Shreds are a quick topping to any taco and can be melted down to make a queso-like sauce.

Fantastic Foods Tofu Scrambler mix Tofu scramble is pretty easy to make, but if you are a particularly lazy vegan, pour a packet of this mix onto a crumbled block of tofu in a cast-iron skillet, and breakfast tacos are done.

Fantastic Foods Taco Filling mix Like the Scrambler mix, but even easier—you just add hot water! It makes a heap of taco meat in minutes. Your college dorm room will never smell the same.

Frozen tater tots Check ingredients, but there are many brands of vegan frozen tater tots. We use these in our Tater Tot-cho Taco, but you can also substitute tater tots in any taco with potatoes. Make a few extra today and save them for breakfast tacos tomorrow.

Gardein Golden Fishless Filets This is one of the most amazing vegetarian products to come out in years. If you haven't tried them, you'll be surprised by how well they mimic fried fish. Pop these in a tortilla with our Tartar Sauce (page 124) and some shredded cabbage.

FINDING SPECIALTY TACO INGREDIENTS

We tried to create our recipes with ingredients that anyone could easily find in their local grocery store or supermarket. We believe the Taco Cleanse is for everyone, regardless of geography. Some items will be easier to locate at health food stores, which are growing in popularity these days and are now in most towns. If you are still having trouble finding ingredients, ordering online might be the best option. Here are some great resources:

MexGrocer This online store has an abundance of taco ingredients, cooking utensils, and tortilla-making equipment. If you are in a taco-deprived area of the world, mexgrocer.com will be your best friend. They ship internationally.

Rabbit Food Grocery Taco scientist Jessica is part owner of this Austin-based vegan grocery store, which sells harder-to-find vegan specialty items. Nearly everything they sell in the shop can be found on their website at rabbitfoodgrocery.com. Outside the United States, there are other vegan grocers who ship, including V Word Market in Toronto and Veganz in Berlin.

Amazon Not surprisingly, Amazon has been increasing its taco ingredient supply in recent years. They understand the growing demand for tacos and taco supplies and have stepped in to help. Head over to amazon.com and click the Grocery section.

Vegan Essentials At this mostly online shopt based in Waukesha, Wisconsin, you can find all kinds of fun taco add-ins. They ship just about anywhere from veganessentials.com.

BUT I DON'T WANT TO GIVE UP MY FAVORITE FOODS!

Thinking about taco cleansing but worried you can't go without pizza? or chocolate? or Chinese food? Don't let cravings for these inferior foods hold you back from achieving the highest levels. The thing is, the taco is an all-embracing food. Your tortilla won't judge you if you wrap it around a slice of olive pizza or a scoop of pad thai. Tacos accept you for who you are. If you're craving . . .

Chinese food: Have you ever had moo shu vegetables? That's the idea. Just be careful with how you fold your tortilla or you might end up with a burrito. Stir-fry veggies (and maybe tofu if you're into that), add a bit of plum sauce, and fill a flour tortilla.

Veggie burgers: Slice up a cooked veggie burger and serve it in a tortilla (corn or flour, it's up to you) with lettuce, tomato, pickles, and your choice of ketchup and/or mustard.

Pad thai (or Thai food in general): Order up some Thai food (or cook it if you're the ambitious type). Put it in a flour tortilla. Eat.

Chocolate: Let me introduce you to the Chocolate-Raspberry Dessert Taco (page 166): a warm waffle folded around your choice of ingredients. It's the best taco choice if you're wanting something sweet.

French fries: Potatoes were pretty much invented for tacos. Stick those bad boys in a taco and eat. French fries go with anything, so use your imagination and go wild.

A burrito: What the hell is wrong with you?

ONE-WEEK MEAL PLAN

If you're having a hard time imagining what it would be like to eat tacos for every meal, that's understandable. Cleansing is hard work! That's why we've provided you with a sample menu for a Hot Taco Cleanse. Obviously it can be adjusted up or down for a Mild, Medium, or Fuego cleanse. Use this meal plan as a guide, not a rule book. Substitute your favorite tacos as you see fit, and don't be concerned about including the sides: As long as your main dish is a taco, all is well.

MONDAY

BREAKFAST

Breakfast taco (see Note on page 23)

LUNCH

Ion-Charged Refried Beans (page 82) or canned vegetarian refried beans and Abundant Roasted Potato (page 74) tacos

Guacamole Viridis (page 126) and tomatoes on a bed of lettuce

DINNER

Burger tacos (veggie burger patty, lettuce, tomato, onions, and pickles on your choice of tortilla)

Carrot sticks with Soothing Jalapeño Ranch (page 123)

SUPPLEMENT

Everyday Mexican Martini (page 181)

TUESDAY

BREAKFAST
Breakfast taco

LUNCH
Foundational Tempeh Bacon (page 105), tomato, and spinach tacos

DINNER
Smoked Brisket and Jalapeño Mac and Cheese Tacos (page 149)
Deeply Roasted Chipotle Butternut Squash (page 72)

SUPPLEMENT
Avocado Margarita (page 177)

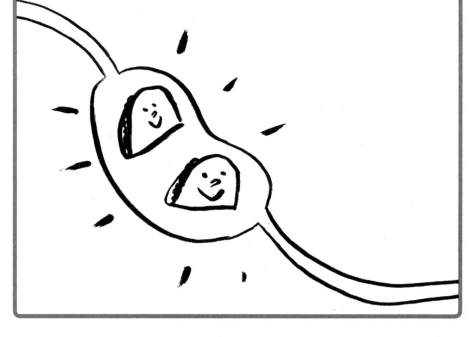

WEDNESDAY

BREAKFAST

Breakfast taco

LUNCH

Deeply Roasted Chipotle Butternut Squash (page 72) and
Foundational Tempeh Bacon (page 105) taco

Enzymatic Escabeche (page 136)

DINNER

Takeout taco: your favorite restaurant food in a tortilla. Our
favorites are Thai and Indian curries, pad thai, and falafel.

SUPPLEMENT

Fundamental Margarita (page 173)

THURSDAY

BREAKFAST

Breakfast taco

LUNCH

Convenience-food taco: your favorite packaged foods in a taco.
We like to use frozen tofu scramble meals, canned chili, and
frozen bean and rice meals. See page 15 for more ideas.

DINNER

Full-Spectrum Tacos (page 138)

SUPPLEMENT

Mind-Limbering Michelada (page 186)

FRIDAY

BREAKFAST

Breakfast taco

LUNCH

Leftovers taco: leftovers from earlier in the week in a taco.

DINNER

Go out for dinner at your favorite taco restaurant.

SUPPLEMENT

Grab a drink while you're out for dinner.

SATURDAY

BREAKFAST

Energizing Dutch Waffle Tacos (page 160)

LUNCH

Tolerant Bulgur Chorizo (page 78) and chickpea tacos

Orange

DINNER

Leftovers or fast-food tacos

SUPPLEMENT

Rehydrating Waterita (page 178)

SUNDAY

BRUNCH

Mighty Migas Tacos (page 95)

Leftover Tolerant Bulgur Chorizo and Abundant Roasted Potatoes
(page 74) on the side

DINNER

Tater Tot-cho Tacos (page 146)

SUPPLEMENT

Agave Margarita (page 174)

NOTE: Breakfast tacos are usually a simple combination of two or three ingredients and possibly a sauce or garnish. Make a big batch of a few ingredients over the weekend, such as Abundant Roasted Potatoes (page 74), Wake and Shake Scramble (page 96), Foundational Tempeh Bacon (page 105), or Radiant Rajas (page 65), and you'll have not only breakfast for the entire week but also a head start on lunch and dinner.

HOW TO GET MORE TACO OPTIONS AT YOUR FAVORITE VEGAN RESTAURANT

We are super lucky to live in Austin, where almost every vegan restaurant has a taco option. There are even a couple of all-taco vegan food trucks here! Since moving to Austin might not be in your five-year plan, here is a guide to getting more taco options in your hometown.

Ask the waitstaff. Your first attempt should be in person at the restaurant. When your server comes to tell you the specials, ask her or him if there are any taco specials tonight. If the server looks puzzled or even laughs, don't be discouraged. You are planting the seeds for a taco harvest later.

Leave a note. A handwritten note in with your check will not go unnoticed. Something such as, "I very much enjoyed my meal tonight. My compliments to the chef! Also, it would be great if you added tacos to your menu, so that I don't have to bring my own tortillas next time."

Get your friends in on it. If you have some taco-cleansing friends, have them call and ask the restaurant if they will have a taco special sometime soon. Mention that "Taco Tuesday" is a thing that people do now.

Speak with the manager. Try to pick a slow night or middle of the afternoon shift to go and speak with the owner, manager, or chef. Bring a copy of this book to show them the delicious tacos they could serve.

Hit them on social media. Every restaurant has Facebook, Instagram, and/or Twitter. Politely post on the restaurant's social media asking when you should expect tacos. Take photos of your own taco creations and hashtag them with #tacocleanse #arentyoujealous

How to Order Vegan Tacos at Taco Bell

You're on a road trip across America, and you need a taco. Taco Bell to the rescue! While it may not be the most vegan-friendly taco establishment you'll ever see, it does have options. Memorizing these tips will make ordering easy.

CRUNCHY TACO — No beef, no cheese, add beans, add rice (or guacamole, tomatoes, etc.), comes with lettuce.

SOFT TACO — No beef, no cheese, add beans, add rice (or guacamole, tomatoes, etc.), comes with lettuce.

There are other, non-taco items that can be made from the Taco Bell menu (such as the 7-LAYER BURRITO minus cheese and sour cream), which makes this fast food restaurant a great place to visit when dining with non-taco cleansing vegan friends! Just remember you can add or subtract from any menu item. Putting in beans, potatoes, and guacamole can add a lot of substance when you've removed the cheese, sour cream, beef, or chicken.

#wishyourrestaurantmadethese and #sorrynotsorry. The more hashtags the better.

When the tacos start appearing, show up and eat them. Have a celebratory meal with your friends when the restaurant finally adds tacos to the menu. Make a big deal about it, and be sure to thank your server and the manager if available. Order as many tacos as possible and rejoice.

Continue to support them or they will go away! This final step is crucial. Eat the tacos from this restaurant as much as you can. There's no way the restaurant will continue to make tacos if no one is ordering them. You must show them your support and continue to spread the word in your community.

TACO JOURNALING

One of the most powerful things you can do in your taco journey is taco journaling. Writing down your thoughts during your Taco Cleanse now will be like having a time machine for your future self. Future You can go back and see how you've changed over time, where you had taco successes and taco failures. Future You will learn from your mistakes, and trust me, you'll be so thankful for that.

Your journal doesn't have to be fancy. You can use an old notebook, some recycled printer paper stapled together, the back pages of an old smartphone manual . . . Or, to be creative and make a store-bought or homemade journal that is special to you, cut out pictures of tacos from your local newspaper or favorite taco magazine and glue them onto the front cover. Write something inspirational on the front page, such as one of the Taco Quotes found inside this book. Every time you open your journal, you will feel peace in your heart.

Commit to daily taco journaling. No one will read your journal, so be free to write whatever comes to mind. Be courageous, because tacos give you courage. Try sitting on a yoga mat and swaddling yourself up in a soft shawl or blanket to mimic the warm feeling of a tortilla. The constant pressure has a calming effect on your bodymind.

Remember, try to write every day, but don't beat yourself up if you miss a day or two. The Taco Cleanse isn't about perfection; it's about expressing your innermost dreams. Write what you want, but consider asking yourself one or more of these questions as you write.

→ How are you feeling today?

→ What tacos have you eaten so far today?

→ What tacos are you most looking forward to eating later?

→ List one fear you used to have that tacos helped cure.

→ Name one person in your life that you believe could be healed with tacos.

→ Did you have a vivid dream last night brought on by spicy salsa?

A Taco Meditation

The tortilla, the circle, the whole, the past and future, folding time, cradling the present moment, channeling nourishment, savoring the now, grasping the continuum firmly yet gently, consuming truth, assimilating innate wisdom.

DEAR TACO SCIENTISTS:
YOUR QUESTIONS ANSWERED

I'm headed out to my cousin's wedding this July. What can I do to avoid eating non-tacos?

Summer weddings require extreme taco creativity. If you are in the bridal party, try keeping a stash of tortillas in your purse. For groomsmen, store tortillas in a cummerbund for use at the buffet. If you're a guest, your best bet is to bring your own tacos (BYOT), wrap them in foil, and leave them on the dashboard of your car. Simply come out during the reception, and they will be hot and ready!

My grandma was confused and made me a burrito. I don't want to hurt her feelings; what do I do?

Turn the burrito into a taco! Easiest way to do this is open the tortilla, scrape out the ingredients onto a plate, and then put them back into the same tortilla—but this time fold it like a taco. Remember—one fold only! Explain this to your grandma, and she will appreciate the lesson in taco science. Another easy way to turn a burrito into a taco is to cut the burrito up into smaller bite-size pieces, and then put the pieces into a separate tortilla. You may need to split it into multiple tortillas. As the saying goes, "Why eat a burrito when you can eat three tacos?"

It's my coworker's day to decide where to eat lunch. What do I do at a salad bar?

Remember your ABCs . . . Always Be Carrying (Tortillas)! You can fill up your tray with lots of veggies, fruit, beans, sometimes even tofu, and then put it all in your tortillas. They may even have salsa.

My boyfriend is a fruitarian. We don't want to uncook two different meals every single day. What can I do to make our mornings easier?

Living with a non-taco-cleanser can be difficult. Try bending to his fruitarian ways by putting a banana and some peanut butter in a tortilla. Bananas are fruit! If peanut butter isn't raw enough, you could put almonds in a Vitamix and use that instead. Cut a collard green leaf into a circle and you have a raw tortilla. Live in harmony!

HOW DO YOU EAT A TACO? ONE BITE AT A TIME.

*What about my dog? I feel
bad getting all the benefits
while my dog is suffering
without tacos.*

Your pup is in luck! We have
a great recipe given to us by
Dinger, one of Stephanie's
beagles. Spread two
tablespoons of peanut butter
on a tortilla. Top with a banana
and a piece of vegetarian jerky
such as a Primal Strip. Sprinkle
with nutritional yeast. Fold
and serve.

*I've heard microwaves are
dangerous. Is that true?*

Absolutely! Never microwave yourself or any other animal no matter
how tempting it is. Plants do great in the microwave, though, and it's
a helpful shortcut to cooking potatoes, melting chocolate, or boiling
water. Don't make the Taco Cleanse harder on yourself by avoiding
this useful cooking tool.

I hate vegetables so how can I eat [this vegetable]?

Why would you torture yourself by eating vegetables that you hate?
Why not eat tacos instead? Did you know that when you cook
the vegetables in the recipes for the Taco Cleanse, they turn into
something amazing? They turn into tacos! Hate eggplants? Turn
them into tacos! What about mushrooms? Make them into tacos!

Harness the transformative power of the Taco Cleanse and break yourself free from the tyranny of vegetable intolerance!

I've started the program but I find myself hungry all the time.

The Taco Cleanse was developed by taco scientists to raise your levels to their highest possible elevation. The more tacos you eat, the faster you will achieve Fuego status. If you are feeling hungry on the Taco Cleanse, you are clearly not eating enough tacos. We would recommend maximizing your daily intake of tacos to heighten the effects.

In my pantry and fridge, I have foods that I want to eat, but I don't know if they are acceptable on the Taco Cleanse. Please help!

We have created an easy-to-remember system to address this type of situation, and we call it: If It Fills Your Tacos (IIFYT). Does the food item in your pantry fit inside a tortilla? Then it is appropriate on the Taco Cleanse. Is the food item too large for a taco and will only fit inside a burrito? Then it is not allowed on the Taco Cleanse. Remember #IIFYT, you can eat it!

Should I get a job at our local vegan taco food truck?

We understand the desire to be around tacos all day. The best vocation is the one that you love, so if you can get a job working with tacos, you should go for it. If there is no local vegan food truck in your area, start your own! Your friends and neighbors will thank you.

I heard that [famous celebrity] was on the Taco Cleanse. Is that true?

Actually, yes, it is true. Most movie stars and celebrities have tried the Taco Cleanse at some point in their careers, and many of them wouldn't even be famous if it weren't for the benefits they received from the Taco Cleanse. But don't blindly follow whatever diet your favorite megastar is promoting at the moment, because once in a while they might eat a burrito, and that's just not right. The Taco Cleanse isn't about celeb worship; it's about doing what's right for you.

Send your burning taco questions to tacocleanse@gmail.com.

> "If people only eat tacos because they fear hunger, then we are a sorry lot indeed."
>
> —EINSTEIN

The BUILDING BLOCKS of a TACO-BASED DIET

BASIC INGREDIENTS
AND THEIR PROPERTIES

Achiote powder or paste (annatto) A common spice blend from Mexico that is also responsible for making rice and other foods red. It can be found at any Mexican store or online.

Agave nectar A syrup made from the agave plant. Find it near the sugar or maple syrup in most grocery stores. The agave plant is what they use to make tequila, so it's obviously a superfood.

Avocados We always use the Hass variety from California. Avocados prevent the organs from drying out and aging. Finding the perfect avocado can be tricky. Sometimes it's easier to get green, hard avocados and just wait for them to ripen. When they start to turn dark green and give a bit when you squeeze lightly, they are ready. Once the skin turns black and the inside is flecked with brown, it's better to just toss them out.

BBQ sauce Breakthrough BBQ Sauce (page 126) is the most powerful. Its formula can be found in the pages of this book. If you absolutely can't manufacture your own, we prefer a Texas variety like Stubb's, which is less sweet than Memphis or Kentucky varieties. Texas sauces can balance out the tempers in your body, while sweeter sauces may overly ignite your passions.

TODAY I ABANDON ALL OLD DIETS AND COMMIT MYSELF FULLY TO THE TACO CLEANSE.

Bulgur If you chop wheat groats into small pieces, parboil them, and then dry them, you end up with bulgur. Don't do all that. Buy it at a store, near the rice. Most people drown it with parsley and call it tabouli. We prefer to dress it with the best spices we can find in recipes like Tolerant Bulgur Chorizo (page 78) and in the chili in our Frito Pie Taco (page 152).

Cashews The secret ingredient to make vegan food creamy, cashews are generally bought raw and then soaked in water for at least two hours before being used in our recipes. There are some claims being made that cashews can be as effective as Prozac and some other antidepressants for lifting your mood, so turn off the Morrissey and eat some cashews instead. Keep a jar in the fridge with soaking nuts for weeks at a time for spontaneous cooking.

Cheese Our helpful friendly book contains two cheese sauces that work for nearly every occasion. When you're short on time, use the Minimalist Nacho Cheese (page 128). When you are feeling like you want to treat your body to luxury, enjoy the Elevated Nacho Cheese (page 130) and let your body be soothed by the added oil. Of course, store-bought vegan cheeses have come a long way and can be substituted as well. Everyone has different preferences when it comes to vegan cheese, but Follow Your Heart, Daiya, and Chao Slices by Field Roast are some of the most popular in the United States. Experiment. Find out which ones you like best.

Chiles

Aji amarillo A pepper native to South America that's ubiquitous in Peruvian cuisine and beloved for its fruity, unique taste. You can buy it in many forms. The paste is easiest to work with, and it keeps in the fridge for a very long time. You can substitute a minced jalapeño if you like. Aji amarillo is delicious cooked with beans, added to Cashew Crema (page 125), or tossed with roasted potatoes.

Anaheim Green chiles grown in New Mexico. If you can't find them fresh they are pretty easy to find in a can labeled "Green Chiles" wherever Mexican food is sold.

Ancho The name given to dried poblanos, these are very common in Mexican cooking. You can order a big bag if you don't have access to Mexican food or dry your own poblanos. Ancho chile powder will also work.

Chipotle in adobo A very common ingredient in Mexican and Tex-Mex cooking usually found in a small can. Chipotles are smoke-dried jalapeños in adobo sauce that add a bit of heat and smokiness to any recipe. Generally you use just a bit, not the whole can. You can freeze tablespoon-size portions, and one can will last you through many recipes.

> "You must make the taco you wish to eat in the world."
>
> —GANDHI

Guajillo Large dried Mexican chile commonly used all over Mexico and the Southwest United States.

Habanero A small fresh pepper that can be green, orange, or red. This is the spiciest pepper we call for, so you can start slow and add more as your tolerance to spice increases.

Hatch One of the most revered peppers in the United States, the Hatch pepper ripens in September in the town of Hatch, New

Mexico, and is worth seeking out in season if you are into that sort of thing. The smell of roasting Hatch peppers will fill your olfactory senses with unique pleasures. If you can't find it you can always substitute another green pepper such as Anaheims, Hungarian wax, or even green bell peppers.

Jalapeño A small spicy pepper used all over the world, the jalapeño is very important to the Taco Cleanse. We call for both fresh and canned, sliced versions in the Taco Cleanse. You can taste a little bit to see how spicy your jalapeño is before you add it, because they can vary quite a bit. If it's too spicy, remove the membranes and seeds.

Pasilla This pepper is sold dried, usually in the produce section of specialty markets or especially taco-friendly grocery stores. When toasted and ground up, it adds a medium-hot, earthy flavor. If you must, substitute ancho chiles.

Poblanos A pleasantly plump poblano pepper, found wherever Mexican ingredients are sold, will make your life better in countless ways. Since this is a more mild pepper, eating it will not only increase your tolerance for spiciness but will also start to awaken the fire in your belly at the *Manipura* chakra.

Chili powder In the United States, chili powder is a blend of ground spices, often including cumin, paprika, cayenne, and oregano. If you can't find chili powder in your country, you can make your own. Combine 2 tablespoons ground mild chiles (ancho, paprika, or your favorite), 1 tablespoon ground cumin, 1 tablespoon oregano, ¾ tablespoon garlic powder, and ½ teaspoon cayenne pepper.

Cilantro Also known as fresh coriander, cilantro is integral to the Taco Cleanse. The chemical compounds in cilantro bind to toxic metals and loosen them from the tissue, so if you've been regularly exposed to mercury, eat this amazing herb. You can find it for very cheap at Mexican or Asian specialty stores, but if there aren't any in your area you can also try growing it; it doesn't need a lot of sun. If you don't like cilantro, you can try substituting basil, mint, scallions, or parsley, BUT a Taco Cleanse may rewrite your genome so that you can enjoy this beautiful foodstuff.

Coconut It has been shown that coconuts slow the progression of and can potentially reverse Alzheimer's and other dementia, so if you are losing your mind, look to coconuts to find it. We use either canned coconut milk or fresh young coconuts in our recipes. The latter can be found at Asian markets or places like Whole Foods. It looks like a white cylinder with a cone-shaped top. The mature version with a brown husk is not used in this book. Coconut water is filled with electrolytes, which is what plants crave.

Epazote This Mexican herb is very popular in Mexico, especially when cooking black beans. You can find it in Mexican specialty food stores and online, and you can grow the seeds. Feel free to leave it out.

Hominy Corn that's dried, soaked, and processed through nixtamalization with an alkaline solution, resulting in an almost bean-like, snappy-textured large corn kernel. You can substitute chickpeas for texture, corn for flavor, or a bit of both if you can't find these in the canned or ethnic food aisle.

Hot dogs Vegetarian versions, like Smart Dogs, abound at most grocery stores in the US at this point. You could also make your own sausages or even substitute a Field Roast–brand sausage if you don't care for hot dogs. The vegan version is free of nitrates or nitrites or whatever those are.

Hot sauce We use several hot sauces in the Taco Cleanse. Frank's RedHot is made in Buffalo, New York, and is where Buffalo sauce gets its flavor. Cholula is made in Mexico and is the most commonly used with Mexican-style tacos. Tabasco is made in Louisiana and is predominantly cayenne and vinegar. It is used in more Southern recipes. Sriracha originates in Thailand and its flavor is predominantly garlic and chiles. Use it in Asian-style recipes or the Sincere Sriracha-Agave Tenders (page 102). Yellowbird is made here in Austin, Texas; it's a mix of carrots, habanero peppers, onions, garlic, tangerine juice, and lime juice and can be used on any taco, because no matter where our tacos get their inspiration, they are all made Austin-style. If you can't find Yellowbird, look for a Scotch bonnet– or habanero–based hot sauce in the Caribbean aisle. If you don't like spicy food, Frank's is the most mild and a good place to start. Your tolerance for spice will go up the more you cleanse.

MAKE TODAY'S TACO AMAZING.

Liquid smoke Pieces of wood from trees like hickory or mesquite are burned, and particles of the smoke are collected in condensers. This results in a liquid that is then concentrated and sold in a tiny bottle. You only need a little bit. It can work as a fumigation for your internal organs, getting rid of "bad" bugs.

Margarine Earth Balance is our preferred brand because it uses no hydrogenated oils and is thus free of trans fats, which is what makes most margarines unhealthy. Margarine can lubricate your mouth and throat, preventing "cotton mouth." If you have a beard, you can use it as a conditioner, for sheen and body. It also tastes great.

PEACE BEGINS WITH TACOS.

Mayo Use our mayo from the Rewarding Esquites recipe (page 68). Alternatively, Follow Your Heart's Vegenaise and Hampton Creek's Just Mayo are both fantastic plant-based versions. They can be found in many grocery stores, including Target and Costco. Vegan mayonnaise has been shown to heal and rejuvenate from the inside and out. One well-known mayo hack is to smear it on your hair to rehome a feral lice colony.

Nutritional yeast Also known as nooch, these yellow flakes can be found at any health food store and are packed with vitamins that will fill you with taco power. Adds a vibrant yellow glow to your urine that resembles the radiance of the sunrise.

Oil We call for a variety of oils, including olive, canola, coconut, peanut, and oil spray—mostly because there are four authors of this book, all with their own preferred oil. Generally, they're interchangeable. But don't waste your good, flavorful extra virgin olive oil on frying or in recipes that will overwhelm its taste (when we call for "cooking oil," we mean "not olive").

Onions White onions are most often used in Mexico, whereas yellow sweet onions are more often used in Texas. We use both interchangeably depending on what we feel drawn to. Use whichever you prefer. Red onions are best for raw applications and pickles. We also use scallions and onion powder on occasion. Onion powder is best in sauces and spice mixes, while scallions are used raw to top everything you eat to add crunch and brightness. Current theories suggest that if you are feeling sick, putting an onion in the room can even absorb the illness.

Oregano, Mexican Although Mexican oregano is in a different botanical family than European oregano, you can substitute one for the other. According to herbalist Charlotte Branca, "In the commencement of measles [oregano] is useful in producing a gentle perspiration and bringing out the eruption, being given in the form of a warm infusion, which is also valuable in spasms, colic, and to give relief from pain in dyspeptic complaints."

Plant milk Some recipes call for specific varieties, but generally soy, almond, or rice milks can all be used interchangeably; just make sure you get an unsweetened variety that's not flavored. Look at the carton ingredients; the kinds with just two ingredients are easiest to work with.

Plantains This cousin of the banana is used throughout the tropical world. The green variety is less sweet and more potato-like. As they turn from yellow to black, they get significantly sweeter, so different

---

Taco Science Vocabulary

TACOriolis — The curving of a TORTILLA that is caused by the Earth's rotation.

TACOndensation — When a SALSA changes state from MILD to SPICY.

TACOnstellation — Patterns formed by groups of TACOS in the sky.

TACOrrelation — The relationship between two TACOS such that knowledge about one TACO can be used to understand another TACO. Remember, Tacorrelation does not imply Tacausation.

recipes call for different levels of ripeness. Plain fried plantains can be either sweet or savory, depending on what you prefer.

Pumpkin seeds Did you ever wonder why people enjoy Halloween so much? It's most likely not because of the costumes and candy but from ingesting pumpkin seeds, which have been shown to increase cosmic healing energy. We use the hulled variety because our time is too important to be spent dealing with pumpkin hulls.

Ro-Tel According to Ro-Tel historians, "Way back in 1943, Carl Roettele had an idea—marry the richness of fresh tomatoes to the zestiness of green chile peppers. The result was legendary and the rest is history." We couldn't agree more. Basically Ro-Tel is canned diced tomatoes with peppers and salt. You can substitute with other brands or fresh ingredients. A typical can of Ro-Tel is just ten ounces, so keep that in mind when substituting other brands.

Sour cream Page 125 has an easy two-ingredient recipe for a homemade *crema*, but it takes a couple of days to ferment. If you need sour cream RIGHT NOW, Tofutti is a good brand to try. We like it on more "meaty" tacos or to cut down spice and drown out the sourness of your soul. It also works nicely with fried foods.

Soy Curls These pieces of dehydrated soy beans can be tough to find but are worth ordering over the Internet because they have a great texture and are quite healthy, providing your RDA of curl. Store them in the fridge for months or the freezer for years. You can substitute seitan in recipes that call for them; just skip the rehydrating process.

> HACK YOUR TACO CLEANSE: Save the bottoms of green onions and keep in a glass of water. They'll regrow forever!

Soy sauce Since soy sauces vary in saltiness quite a bit, we tested these recipes with Kikkoman soy sauce or tamari, which is available everywhere. Getting enough salt in the Taco Cleanse is important because it draws out dihydrogen monoxide from your cells and increases your thirst for Supplements.

Tamarind This tropical fruit is commonly dried before it's sold. Tamarind in the pod is kind of a pain to use, so it is commonly found as a paste or pulp. Find it in Southeast Asian or Central American grocery stores.

Tempeh A slab of fermented soy that we enjoy for both its high protein content, which is good for taco power, and its taste. It can be found in the refrigerated section of most health food stores and larger grocery stores. Tempeh is loaded with enzymes that cultivate your gut flora and fauna.

Tequila Like champagne or cognac, tequila can only be made from a specific region in Mexico. The unaged silver (*plata* or *blanco*) is appropriate for all the recipes in this book. The more tequila is aged, the more it takes on the characteristics of the wood barrels it is aged in, so for shots you may enjoy *reposado, añejo*, and *extra añejo*, but these expensive varieties are not necessary. However, make sure you don't get a really cheap bottle; the cheaper the bottle, the more impure the liquor and the more likely you are to consume impurities. Ask someone at the liquor store to help you find a good silver that will fit your budget.

Tofu The extra-firm variety, packed in water, in the refrigerated section of most grocery stores, is the best one to buy for these recipes. Like a chameleon, tofu will mirror any healing benefits projected on it.

Tomatillos Resembling green tomatoes in paper jackets, tomatillos are used to make salsa verde and other green sauces. When cooking with fresh tomatillos, remove the paper jackets and wash off the sticky substance that clings to the skin. You can also purchase tomatillos canned. Green foods are packed with chlorophyll, which converts sunshine into nourishment. It's nature's solar panel. When you eat green foods, the sun will grow in your heart.

Vegetable broth We call for a variety of vegetable broths in the book. You can find these at the health food store in powder, cube, or liquid form, but often regular grocery stores carry them as well. We use the Goya Ham Flavored Concentrate and Better Than Bouillon No Chicken flavor the most. A standard vegetarian powder is also called for.

Vital wheat gluten The major ingredient in homemade seitan, vital wheat gluten is made by isolating the gluten from flour. You can do this yourself by repeatedly washing regular flour, but we prefer to buy the Bob's Red Mill Variety that can be found in most health food stores. Although it's an ancient superfood, gluten has a bad reputation these days, but we are working to prove it's the glue that holds our bodies together.

Q: Why are pequin peppers so HOT?

A: Because otherwise they'd be a little chile.

Troubleshooting Your Taco Cleanse

Sometimes people write the Institute of Taco Science saying, "I did a Taco Cleanse and nothing happened. What's the big idea?" Most often the problem comes down to one of three things:

1 YOU'RE NOT ACTUALLY EATING A TACO. Filling + condiments + tortilla = taco, right? Not exactly. There are many taco-like objects out there waiting to trip up the novice taco cleanser. The most common of these is the burrito. You can recognize a burrito by its mulitple folded edges (versus a taco's single fold) and its generally large size. Burritos often require a two-handed hold, whereas the average taco only requires a single hand (which hand you use is up to you). See our guide to What Is a Taco? on page 5. SOLUTION: Eat a damn taco!

2 YOU'RE NOT CLEANSING LONG ENOUGH. At any level below "mild" (one full day of taco meals), you're unlikely to see any visible changes. You can't just supplement one taco a month and expect to see big results. What you get out of the cleanse depends on what you put into it. Turn to page 3 and refresh yourself on the four levels of taco cleansing. SOLUTION: Eat more tacos!

3 YOU'RE NOT ALIVE. Taco cleansing is not recommended for zombies or the undead. SOLUTION: None. There's no point in trying to live a tacoless existence.

TORTILLAS

If you only take away one thing from the Taco Cleanse, it should be the importance of the tortilla. There is no taco without the tortilla. It protects the delicate skin of your hands from the hot fillings. It shelters your phytonutrients from the harsh elements of your plate. Many plates are made of toxic substances like melamine or bleached paper. The tortilla is portable. It's soft like your mother's bosom. Except when it's crunchy, like your father's beard. It's biodegradable, eco-friendly, and of the highest vibration. Above all, it's delicious.

The tortilla is adaptable: Make yours from wheat, corn, collard greens, plantains, or pure love. Wheat tortillas are known for their durability and flexibility. Use a flour tortilla if you're making your taco in advance. Corn is more delicate and elusive. Its properties quickly deteriorate. Eat fresh corn tortillas as soon as possible.

This chapter also includes tortilla-like objects. Purists might say they're not actually tortillas, but the Taco Cleanse isn't about perfection. It's about being awesome. Some fillings have an affinity for specific "tortillas." Crunchy vegetables pair well with a collard tortilla. And what's a dessert taco without a waffle tortilla?

Above all, remember the famous words of Hippocrates: "If there's more than one fold, it's a burrito."

FLOUR TORTILLAS

Makes about twenty 6-inch (15 cm) tortillas

THIS RECIPE COMES TO US from an ancient family recipe belonging to Crystal Tate. And like the white agate crystal itself, these tortillas are grounding and will fill your bodymind with clarity.

1 In a bowl, combine the flour, baking powder, and salt. Using a fork or the tips of your fingers, add in the margarine. Slowly add the water, kneading the dough gently until everything combines into a nice, pretty ball of dough. If the dough is sticky, add additional flour, one tablespoon at a time. If it won't form a smooth ball, add more water, 1 tablespoon at a time. Place the ball of dough in a bowl and cover with a plate or damp towel. Let the dough rest for 20 minutes.

2 Divide the dough into about 20 equal-size balls. Working on a lightly floured surface, flatten each ball and then roll out into 6-inch (15 cm) circles. Heat a skillet,

4 cups (480 g) all-purpose flour, plus more for rolling out tortillas

2 teaspoons baking powder

1 teaspoon salt

6 tablespoons vegan margarine, such as Earth Balance

About 1¼ cups (300 ml) warm water

comal, or grill on medium-high heat. Cook each tortilla on one side for about a minute, until you see light brown spots. Flip the tortilla over to cook for another 30 seconds or so. Store in a covered container in the refrigerator for a few days or, with pieces of parchment paper or wax paper between the tortillas, in the freezer for several months.

SUPER CLEANSE: It's easy to find vegan tortillas at the store, but check the ingredients because fillers do tend to get added more to flour than corn.

CORN TORTILLAS,
OPPOSITE PAGE

FLOUR TORTILLAS,
PAGE 47

CORN TORTILLAS

Makes twelve 6-inch (15 cm) tortillas

MAKING YOUR OWN TORTILLAS is life-changing. Sandra, mid-thirties massage therapist said, "If there is one thing I regret in this life, it's that I didn't start making corn tortillas earlier." Once you get the hang of it, making them is much easier than buying them at the store, and infinitely more delicious.

Corn tortillas are made from dried corn that's been treated with an alkalizing agent that removes the husks. Theoretically you can do this yourself to make fresh masa (dough), but it is much easier to buy "instant masa" or, *en español*, "masa harina." Maseca is the most popular brand, but if you feel like splurging, Bob's Red Mill makes one, too. The recipe is on the back of the bag, but it's really one of those things that you have to get a feel for. The key is to use warm water and add a little bit at a time until the dough comes together. If you add too much water, it will stick to your hands, so just add more masa. If you add too much masa, it won't hold together. If this happens, add more water.

2 cups (224 g) masa harina

½ teaspoon salt

1½ to 2 cups (360 to 480 ml) warm water

1 Combine the masa harina and the salt with a fork in a medium mixing bowl. Begin to add warm water, a half cup at a time and mix it with clean hands until it's no longer powdery; this will take a bit of practice, but once you've done it a couple of times, you'll know when you've added enough water. If it's sticky, that means you've added too much water; add a bit more masa harina.

2 Once the masa has come together, let it rest while you heat up your skillet to medium heat. If you have a smooth griddle or a traditional comal, you can make your tortillas on that. Otherwise, use a heavy cast-iron skillet. Note that you do not use any oil in corn tortillas. Cut two pieces of plastic to be a bit larger than your 6-inch tortillas. I use a plastic ziplock bag, but you could also use a grocery bag or similar.

(Recipe continues . . .)

3 Divide the dough into 12 balls and press the balls in between the pieces of plastic. You can do this with a tortilla press or even use a heavy pot. Peel one piece of plastic off and then place the tortilla in your hand. Slowly peel off the other piece of plastic and gently place the dough round on the hot griddle. Let it cook until the edges start to turn color, about 30 seconds to a minute, and then flip the tortilla. Hopefully it will puff up; if not, it will still be good. Cook it for another minute or so and place in either a tortilla warmer, a towel, or foil and then repeat with the remaining dough balls.

TIP You can buy a tortilla warmer that you pop tortillas into as you are making them, or you could also wrap them in foil and keep them in a warm oven.

PLANTAIN TORTILLAS

Makes about ten 6-inch (15 cm) tortillas

3 green plantains

1 teaspoon salt

Cooking oil spray

IF YOU CAN'T EAT GRAINS LIKE WHEAT OR PSEUDOGRAINS LIKE CORN, you can still enjoy the many benefits of a taco-based diet by trying this recipe for tortillas made out of plantains. We saw the technique on a blog run by Robb Wolf, and we were inspired to add our own version here so that nothing will stand between you and a taco. This recipe is a lot messier than the other tortilla recipes, and it's a bit difficult to get everything to hold together in a perfect circle, but they are super tasty and a great alternative. They don't keep in the fridge very well, so try to eat them all in one sitting. Eating ten tacos at once can't be wrong.

1 Fill a large pot with water, cover it, and place on a burner to boil. Cut the plantains into thirds, leaving the peels on.

(Recipe continues . . .)

Once the water comes to a boil, add the plantains and ½ teaspoon of the salt and boil away for about 20 minutes. When the skins split, remove the plantains and let cool in a strainer, keeping the pot of hot water on the stove, covered, but with the heat off.

2 Prepare your tortilla press by cutting two pieces of plastic, like a ziplock bag, to be a bit larger than your 6-inch tortillas. Once the plantains are cool enough to handle, slide the peels off and put the flesh in a bowl with the remaining ½ teaspoon salt. Mash with a potato masher or fork. Add a bit of water from the reserved pot to the mash until your plantains resemble

a soft dough. If the dough is too crumbly, add 1 to 2 tablespoons cornstarch or tapioca starch.

3 Heat a griddle, comal, or cast-iron skillet and spray with oil. Roll a small ball in your hand and then place in the tortilla press between the pieces of plastic. Press out a tortilla and carefully peel one piece of plastic off and then place the tortilla in your hand. Slowly peel off the other piece of plastic and gently place the dough round on the hot griddle. Cook one side until the edges start to turn up, about 2 minutes. Flip and cook for another 2 minutes or so. Store in a warmed oven or a tortilla warmer until ready to eat.

COLLARD TORTILLA

Makes 1 tortilla

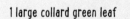

1 large collard green leaf

THIS RECIPE IS VORTEX-INDUCED and proven to make your tacos 70 percent more leafy.

1 Trim any thick stem. Using a 6-inch (15 cm) plate and a sharp knife, cut out a circle in the collard leaf.

WAFFLE TORTILLAS

Makes 4 waffle tortillas

THIS WAFFLE TORTILLA WAS CREATED FOR THE ENERGIZING DUTCH WAFFLE TACOS (page 160), but don't let that stop you from waffle-taco-ing everything in sight. We recommend ice cream, caramelized fruit, or anything battered and fried. Or compound the waffling by cooking tofu and hash brown potatoes in your waffle iron. See Jessica and Wes's Maximum Salad YouTube channel for more ideas of foods to cook in a waffle iron.

1 Whisk the flour, sugar, baking powder, and salt in a large bowl and set aside. Whisk the remaining ingredients in a separate large bowl and wait 5 minutes for the flaxseed to thicken the liquid. Sprinkle the flour mixture into the liquid mixture while incorporating them with a rubber spatula until the batter is just combined. Prepare the waffles according to the waffle iron manufacturer's directions.

1½ cups (180 g) all-purpose flour
1 tablespoon sugar
1 teaspoon baking powder
1 teaspoon salt
1 cup (240 ml) soy milk
¾ cup (180 ml) water
¼ cup (60 ml) canola oil
1 tablespoon ground flaxseed
1 teaspoon apple cider vinegar
½ teaspoon vanilla extract

"Until one has loved a taco, a part of one's soul remains unawakened."
—ANATOLE FRANCE

FILLINGS

The fillings are the grounding components of tacos. When you listen to your body's inner monologue, it cries out for beans, seitan, tofu, tempeh, Soy Curls, vegetables, mushrooms, and fruits. Don't be bound by societal taco norms of breakfast tacos in the morning and dessert tacos only after you finish your taco vegetables. Our motto: Breakfast tacos served all day.

A tortilla without fillings is like a flag without wind. Choose your fillings carefully. Do not be greedy and overfill your taco. Create a safe space where a few well-chosen fillings can work together in harmony. Choose a diversity of fillings: Hot, cold. Crispy, soft. Spicy, cooling. Creamy, acidic.

Many of the fillings can be made in advance, but often we've listed store-bought substitutes. When you eat tacos for every meal, sometimes you need a quick or easy option. The Taco Cleanse isn't about breaking your back cooking. It's about eating tacos.

BRIGHT LIGHT BAJA SLAW

Fills 12 tacos

IT IS PARAMOUNT TO MAINTAIN POSITIVITY during your taco journey. The citric acid provided by the orange juice in this slaw tenderizes the cabbage and wards off negative thoughts. Combine with Iridescent Fried Tofu (page 92) to shine a light on your psychic path. Make ahead and keep refrigerated so the dressing has time to fully energize the cabbage.

1 For the dressing, vigorously whisk the orange juice, oil, jalapeño, agave nectar, spices, and salt together in a large bowl until emulsified. The dressing should look creamy and the oil should no longer separate from the other ingredients. At that point, set it aside.

Juice of 1 large orange
2 tablespoons olive oil
1 jalapeño, seeded and minced
1 tablespoon agave nectar
1 teaspoon coriander seeds, ground
1 teaspoon cumin
½ teaspoon black pepper
¼ teaspoon salt
1 small head of red cabbage

2 Quarter the cabbage along the stem with a large knife. Remove the core from each cabbage wedge with an angled cut and discard. Place the cabbage wedges flat side down and julienne (thinly slice). Move the shredded cabbage to the bowl and toss with the prepared dressing until completely coated.

TROPICAL CEVICHE

Fills 8 tacos

THE SUNNY DAYS AND HUMID NIGHTS of the tropics inspired this take on ceviche. Sometimes, people from the US travel to tropical islands to cure a "brain cloud," but eating this ceviche will have the same effect. It's the perfect recipe for when it's too hot to cook anything; you can let the acidity of the lime do the cooking for you. Serve with plenty of sliced avocado or Cashew Crema (page 125) and hot sauce on a Corn Tortilla (page 49) or Collard Tortilla (page 52). Use the latter and you won't even have to turn the stove on.

1 young coconut
8 ounces (227 g) oyster mushrooms
1 small mango, diced
1 jalapeño, seeded and diced finely
1 medium red onion, diced
¼ cup (60 ml) fresh squeezed orange juice
¼ cup (60 ml) fresh squeezed lime juice
1 teaspoon lime zest
1 tablespoon aji amarillo or jalapeño puree
1 teaspoon salt
⅓ cup (15 g) cilantro, chopped

1 Step 1 is to open the young coconut, which is the hardest part of the whole recipe. If you have a cleaver, that will work great. Essentially you want to split the coconut and save the juice. Then you can scoop out the flesh with a spoon. Chop it into bite-size pieces.

2 Clean the mushrooms with a damp paper towel and cut the heads away from the stems. You can save the stems for stock or another use. Put the coconut, mushrooms, and all remaining ingredients except the cilantro in a bowl. Gently fold everything together. Refrigerate 2 hours and add in the cilantro.

JACKFRUIT BRISKET

Fills 6 tacos

THIS IS THE BRISKET RECIPE you've been searching for all your life. So check that off your bucket list. Jackfruit is commonly used in Southeast Asian cooking. It comes in two varieties: sweet mature fruit in syrup and young green fruit in brine. You want to use the young jackfruit in brine for this recipe. Look for it at Southeast Asian markets or specialty stores like Whole Foods, or substitute 2 cups shredded seitan.

One 20-ounce (565 g) can green jackfruit in brine

1 tablespoon canola oil

½ yellow onion, chopped

1 garlic clove, chopped

1 cup (240 ml) beef-style vegan broth

¼ cup (60 ml) Breakthrough BBQ Sauce (page 126) or store-bought Texas-style BBQ sauce

2 teaspoons soy sauce

1 teaspoon Spirited Salsa Inglesa (page 116) or vegan Worcestershire sauce

½ teaspoon liquid smoke

1 bay leaf

½ teaspoon paprika

¼ teaspoon black pepper

¼ teaspoon cayenne

1 Drain and rinse the jackfruit. Flake the jackfruit with a fork or your hands until it looks like shredded meat. Squeeze as much liquid out of it as possible.

2 Heat the oil in a saucepan over medium heat. Sauté the onion until softened, 2 to 3 minutes. Add the garlic and sauté for 30 seconds. Add the rest of the ingredients and bring to a simmer.

3 Simmer for 20 minutes, or until all the liquid is absorbed. Remove the bay leaf before serving.

BARBACOA MUSHROOMS

Fills 8 tacos

BRAISING IS THE IDEAL COOKING METHOD for mushrooms because it allows the mushrooms to absorb the optimum amount of phytocarbons from the spices. And, as everyone knows, phytocarbons help toxins escape through the rigid cell walls of red blood cells. Serve these in corn tortillas with cilantro and chopped onion.

1 Combine the onion, garlic, chipotle, adobo sauce, pasilla pepper if using, broth, vinegar, lime juice, cumin, oregano, allspice, and cloves in a blender and blend until smooth.

2 Place the mushrooms, bay leaves, and sauce in a sauté pan and bring to a boil. Reduce the heat to low and simmer for 30 minutes, or until the mushrooms are tender and the sauce has thickened and darkened in color. Remove the bay leaves before serving.

½ medium red onion, roughly chopped

5 garlic cloves

1 chipotle in adobo, plus 1 tablespoon adobo sauce

1 dried pasilla pepper, rehydrated in warm water, optional

½ cup (120 ml) vegetable or mushroom broth

2 tablespoons apple cider vinegar

1 tablespoon lime juice

2 teaspoons ground cumin

1 teaspoon oregano

½ teaspoon ground allspice

¼ teaspoon ground cloves

1 pound (454 g) button mushrooms, sliced

2 bay leaves

"The only thing to fear is running out of tacos."
—FRANKLIN DELANO ROOSEVELT

SALSA VERDE,
SEE TIP ON PAGE 114

BARBACOA
MUSHROOMS,
OPPOSITE PAGE

BEER-BATTERED PORTOBELLOS

Fills 16 tacos

WE TALK A LOT IN THE TACO CLEANSE about the importance of tequila, but other alcoholic beverages are great, too. Beer is one of the most ancient elixirs used to help people deal with their feelings. Serve these on a Flour Tortilla (page 47) with french fries and malt vinegar.

1 Pour a 1½-inch (4 cm) layer of oil into a deep pot. Heat the oil to 375°F (190°C). (If you don't have a candy or frying thermometer, throw in a pinch of batter. The oil is hot enough if the batter sizzles and is immediately surrounded with bubbles.) In the meantime, line a baking sheet with paper towels.

2 To make the batter, mix together the flour, baking powder, and salt, then add the beer and mix again. Coat a mushroom slice in the batter and place it in the hot oil with a slotted spoon. Repeat until the pot has mushroom slices in one layer with space between all of them. After one side

Cooking oil

1½ cups (180 g) all-purpose flour

1½ teaspoons baking powder

½ teaspoon salt

12 ounces (355 ml) beer

4 portobello mushrooms sliced into 1-inch (2.5 cm) wide strips

of each mushroom is browned, flip it to cook the other side. Remove the mushrooms one at a time and place on the prepared baking sheet. You will have to do several batches depending on how big your pot is. Eat these as soon as possible for maximum crunchiness.

TIP Watching your oil consumption? Don't make Beer-Battered Portobellos! But consider why you are watching your oil consumption. Did you discuss it with your doctor or nutritionist? If not, maybe you should rethink it. After all, you only live once, and if you want to be happy in that time, eating deep-fried mushrooms might help.

SUPER CLEANSE: Gardein Golden Fishless Filets could be substituted for these portobellos.

EUPHORIC AVOCADO WEDGES

Fills 8 tacos

STUDIES SHOW THAT AVOCADO CONSUMERS are healthier than people who don't eat avocados. According to our own research, they are happier, too. These wedges are packed with happy fats *and* happy carbs: panko bread crumbs have been shown to be 80 percent more jovial than the standard American crumb. Serve the wedges with a happy protein such as seitan, tempeh, or tofu.

1 Preheat the oven to 450°F (230°C). Oil a baking sheet.

2 Prepare three shallow bowls for the breading process. In the first, whisk together the flour, half of the salt, and half of the pepper. In the second, whisk together the soy milk and mustard. In the third, whisk together the panko with the remaining salt and pepper.

3 Cut the avocados in half and remove the pit. Slice both halves in half again to form large wedges. Cut each large wedge lengthwise into three slices. Liberate the

Cooking oil
½ cup (60 g) all-purpose flour
1 teaspoon salt
1 teaspoon black pepper
½ cup (120 ml) unsweetened soy milk
¼ cup (60 ml) prepared brown mustard
1½ cups (90 g) panko bread crumbs
2 medium avocados

slices from the avocado skin by peeling the skin back and down the length of the slices. Dredge each slice through the flour bowl first, then the soy milk bowl, and finally the panko bowl. The slices should be coated completely at each stage. Arrange the coated slices in a single layer on the baking sheet. Bake for 20 minutes, flipping the wedges once halfway through.

TIP Mastery of the ancient dry-hand/ wet-hand technique is highly encouraged. Use one hand when dredging the flour and panko bowls and the other when dipping into the soy milk bowl. This display of coordination promotes a flow state. Lack of focus will result in doughy fingertips. See Iridescent Fried Tofu (page 92) for more detailed instructions.

RADIANT RAJAS

Fills 8 tacos

RAJAS ARE SIMPLY COOKED STRIPS OF PEPPERS
that you will find at any decent taco truck.
They are great in breakfast tacos with tofu
scramble or potatoes, but you can really
add them anywhere. Some restaurants
make them *"con crema,"* so make sure to
ask about dairy before ordering them at a
restaurant. You can also add mushrooms
into the sauté if you want a substantial
filling instead of a topping. Remember, a
spicy pepper can stoke the fire in the belly.

1 Move the oven rack to the highest
position and turn on the broiler. Once
it's hot, put the whole poblanos on a
baking sheet under the broiler. Turn the
peppers over with tongs every 2 minutes,
broiling until they are charred on all sides.
This will take between 10 and 30 minutes.
You can also do this step directly over a
flame if you have a gas burner or a fire.

2 Place the poblanos in a brown school
lunch bag or a small covered container.
They need to steam up a bit so that their
skins will get loose. After 10 minutes put

4 poblano peppers (other peppers will
   work; experiment!)

1 tablespoon cooking oil

1 white onion

2 garlic cloves, chopped

2 teaspoons dried Mexican oregano

½ cup (120 ml) broth or unsweetened plant
   milk

½ teaspoon salt

some gloves on and rub off the skins.
Some remaining skin bits are fine. Cut the
stem off the pepper, slice the pepper in
half, and remove the seeds. Cut the pepper
into strips.

3 Warm up a cast-iron skillet over
medium heat. Add the oil and after
it shimmers, add the onions. When
the onions start to brown, after about 5
minutes, add the garlic, oregano, and
poblano strips and cook for another 2
minutes. Add the broth and let most of
it cook off, 5 to 10 minutes, then remove
from heat.

ZUCCHINI FRITTERS

Fills 8 tacos

SINCE ANCIENT TIMES, people native to the Western Hemisphere have grown corn, squash, and beans all together. The beans climb the cornstalk and the squash shades the ground, providing a living mulch. The beans add nitrogen to the soil as natural fertilizer. These fritters will thus connect you to a long chain of humans living in harmony with the earth and cultivate an attitude of gratitude that will cleanse your inner life.

3 large zucchini or summer squash, shredded (about 4 cups or 560 g)

½ teaspoon salt

4 cups (120 g) cornflakes

15 ounces (425 g) white butter beans, rinsed if canned

1½ teaspoons creole seasoning, such as Tony's

1 tablespoon lemon juice

1 tablespoon nutritional yeast

1 cup (120 g) corn kernels

Cooking oil spray

1 Preheat the oven to 400°F (200°C). Line a baking sheet with a silicone baking mat or parchment paper.

2 Put the shredded zucchini into a colander. Sprinkle some salt on it and let the water drain off while you prepare everything else. Put the cornflakes in a large bowl and mash them into crumbs with a potato masher. In a separate medium bowl, mash up the butter beans with the potato masher. Mix in the creole seasoning, lemon juice, and nutritional yeast. Fold in the corn kernels.

3 Wring out the water from the remaining zucchini by wrapping the shreds in a paper towel and squeezing, then fold the zucchini into the mashed bean mixture. Scoop ¼ cup of the mixture,

roll it into a ball with your hands, and give it a little squeeze. Drop the ball into the cornflake crumbs and roll it around until covered in the cornflakes. Place it on the baking sheet, flattening just a bit. Repeat until you have used all the ingredients. Spray the tops with oil and pop the sheet in the oven. Bake for 45 minutes.

FRIED PLANTAINS

Fills 4 to 8 tacos

2 yellow plantains
Cooking oil for frying

AH, *PLÁTANOS*. These savory bananas beloved throughout the tropical world can be one of the tastiest ingredients around. Studies show they can make you smarter, happier, and more energetic. They even keep you cool on a hot day. Fonzie cool. We like them fried, but if you prefer you can steam them. Remember that plantains can protect you from bone-itis. Serve alongside tofu scramble, Gallo Pinto (page 88), any bean recipe, or with just Guacamole Viridis (page 126) on a corn tortilla.

1 Slice the plantains at an angle to around ½ inch (1.25 cm) thickness. Heat ¼ inch of oil in a pan until a drop of water bubbles furiously once added. Add the plantains and fry on each side about 3 minutes. Remove to paper towels to drain and serve immediately or keep in the oven on its lowest setting until you are ready.

REWARDING ESQUITES

Fills 16 tacos

DID YOU KNOW THAT CORN has the ability to convert sunlight into stored energy? This process is called photosynthesis. Bright yellow corn contains the most bioavailable sunlight. The optimal way to incorporate its radiant effects into a taco-based diet is by making esquites. Like its on-the-cob relative, an elote, esquites is roasted corn kernels accompanied by mayo, chili powder, and lime juice. Unlock the potential of esquites alongside Artisan Seitan Strips (page 112).

For the mayo:

It's best to use a quart-sized, wide-mouth mason jar and an immersion blender. Alternately, a food processor or blender will work, but the oil might not emulsify quite as well. In the mason jar, add the lime juice and soy milk. Insert the immersion blender into the jar. With the immersion blender running at its fastest speed, pour the oil in a constant, thin stream into the

Mayo

2 tablespoons lime juice

½ cup (120 ml) unsweetened soy milk

1 cup (240 ml) canola oil

1 tablespoon agave nectar

¼ teaspoon black pepper

¼ teaspoon salt

8 ears of corn, husks and silk removed

Canola oil cooking spray

2 tablespoons nutritional yeast

1 teaspoon chili powder

jar as slowly as humanly possible. Take this opportunity to practice your breathing. In a couple of minutes, the liquid will thicken into the familiar mayo consistency. Add the agave nectar, pepper, and salt to the jar and give it one more quick blend.

To roast the corn:

Set your oven to its broil setting. Lightly mist the ears of corn with cooking spray and arrange on a cooking sheet. Roast the corn on the oven's center rack for 12 to 15 minutes, rotating the ears every

(Recipe continues . . .)

3 to 5 minutes. When the kernels have roasted, remove the corn from the oven and allow it to cool enough to handle. Cut the stem off of the cob and hold the corn vertically, cut side down, in a shallow bowl. Remove the kernels from the cob using a downward sawing motion with a sharp knife. Repeat for the other ears. Stir in 1 cup (240 ml) of mayo. Garnish with the nutritional yeast and chili powder.

OPTIMAL COCONUT-ROASTED ACORN SQUASH

Fills 8 tacos

1 acorn squash

2 tablespoons of coconut oil

½ teaspoon salt

½ teaspoon black pepper

AS WITH DELICATA SQUASH, you can actually eat the acorn squash peel. Since peeling a squash is the most difficult part about working with one, you can bust out this recipe in no time flat. Or about 30 minutes.

1 Preheat the oven to 400°F (200°C). Line a baking sheet with a silicone baking mat or parchment paper.

2 Put the acorn squash on a cutting board and cut in half. I find the easiest way to do this is with a swift chop of a cleaver (have a first aid kit on hand if you're inexperienced). Remove the seeds and cut the squash into somewhat uniform 2-inch (5 cm) cubes. Move the squash to the prepared baking sheet. Spoon the coconut oil into your clean hand and hold it for a few seconds to soften. Using your hands, rub the oil into the squash flesh and peel. Season with salt and pepper and roast in the oven for 20 minutes. Flip the pieces of squash and bake for another 10 minutes, or until browned.

GROUNDING SWEET POTATO FRIES

Fills 8 tacos

THE HUMBLE SWEET POTATO retains its vibrant orange flesh despite its subterranean habitat. When we find ourselves flying high on Taco Cleanse vibrations, we look to the sweet potato's grounding nature for stability on our journey. Focus on your root chakra while enjoying these baked fries to explore the deepest connections to your physical body.

1 Preheat the oven to 450°F (230°C). Oil a baking sheet.

2 Whisk together 2 tablespoons of oil, the spices, and salt in a large bowl. Slice the sweet potatoes into ¼ inch x ¼-inch (0.5 x 0.5 cm) strips and hand toss them in the bowl with the oil mixture until evenly coated. Arrange the sweet potato strips in a single layer on the prepared baking sheet. Bake for 40 minutes, flipping the strips once halfway through.

2 tablespoons olive oil, plus more for baking sheet

½ teaspoon garlic powder

½ teaspoon ground cumin

½ teaspoon onion powder

½ teaspoon paprika

½ teaspoon black pepper

½ teaspoon salt

2 medium sweet potatoes

"If taquerias had glass walls, then everyone would be taco cleansing."

—LINDA McCARTNEY

DEEPLY ROASTED CHIPOTLE BUTTERNUT SQUASH

Fills 6 to 8 tacos

1 butternut squash

2 teaspoons minced chipotle in adobo

1 tablespoon olive oil

One 15.5-ounce (439 g) can chickpeas

½ teaspoon salt

½ cup (60 g) walnut pieces

ORANGE IS THE COLOR OF CREATIVITY, JOY, and enthusiasm. Add some of this butternut squash to your tacos if you are feeling unfulfilled. It goes great with black beans and Cilantro-Avocado Tranquility Sauce (page 122).

1 Preheat the oven to 400°F (200°C). Line a baking sheet with a silicone baking mat or parchment paper.

2 Slice the butternut squash in half, splitting the bulb from the narrower part. Slice the bulb in half and scoop out the seeds. Trim the peel off all parts and slice into ½-inch (1.25 cm) cubes and place in a large bowl. Whisk together the chipotle in adobo and the oil in a small bowl. Cover the squash with the oil mix and combine with the chickpeas. Spread the mixture on the baking sheet and sprinkle with salt. Bake for 20 minutes, flipping halfway through. The squash is done when it's soft all the way through.

3 While the squash roasts, toast the walnuts in a dry skillet over medium heat for 1 to 2 minutes until they smell fragrant. Remove the skillet from the heat once the nuts are toasted so they don't burn. Mix the walnuts with the squash and chickpeas before serving.

ABUNDANT ROASTED POTATOES

Fills 8 to 10 tacos

2 large russet potatoes

2 tablespoons cooking oil (or enough oil to coat)

1 tablespoon chopped garlic

Salt and black pepper to taste

LIKE PEPPERS, CORN, TOMATOES, AND PEANUTS, the amazing vegetable known as the potato was first born in the Americas. The fastest and easiest way to get it from nubby root to delicious taco filling is to wash it, cut it into cubes, and roast it. Experiment with different spices; smoked paprika is great with a breakfast taco, and oregano would work great with most of the bean recipes. Since garlic goes with just about everything, that's the version used here.

1 Preheat the oven to 400°F (200°C) and line a baking sheet with a silicone baking mat or parchment paper.

2 Clean the potatoes and slice them into ¼-inch (0.5 cm) cubes. Put the potatoes in a pile in the center of the baking sheet.

Pour the oil, garlic, salt, and pepper on top and mix everything together with your hands until the potatoes are well coated. Place in the oven until they are starting to brown, about 20 minutes, then flip the potatoes and roast for another 20 minutes, or until browned.

SUPER CLEANSE: If you can't deal with slicing another potato, you can buy preroasted ones at the grocery store or—a favorite in our laboratory—the mighty tater tot.

AFFIRMATION CUMIN-ONION RICE

Makes 4 cups

IN THE BEANS-AND-RICE COMBO, beans usually bring all the flavor. The rice deserves some love, too. Next time you're feeling inadequate, make this rice and say to yourself, "Like rice, I too deserve love."

1 Heat the oil in a small saucepan over medium heat. Add the cumin seeds and cook, stirring occasionally, for 1 minute. Add the onion and cook until softened, about 3 minutes. Add the rice, stir, and cook for 2 minutes. Add the broth and the salt, if you're using it, and bring everything to a boil. Reduce the heat to low, cover, and cook for 15 minutes.

2 Remove the saucepan from the heat and leave covered for 5 minutes. Fluff with a fork before serving with your favorite beans.

1 tablespoon canola oil

1 teaspoon cumin seeds

½ medium onion, sliced

1 cup (180 g) long grain rice, such as Texmati

2 cups (480 ml) chicken-style vegetable broth

¼ teaspoon salt, optional

"If all you have is a tortilla, everything looks like a taco."

—PROVERB

ARROZ VERDE

Makes 4 cups (960 ml)

GREEN IS THE COLOR OF SPRING, which means it is also the color of growth and rebirth. You will probably experience so much growth during the Taco Cleanse that you will be several inches taller when you are done.

This recipe was inspired by Diana Kennedy's *arroz verde* from her book *The Essential Cuisines of Mexico*. It calls for Hatch chiles, but any other pepper, such as poblanos or serranos, will work; some will be spicy and some won't, so choose accordingly. Serve this green rice on corn tortillas with Ion-Charged Refried Beans (page 82), avocado, and salsa verde.

3 roasted Hatch peppers, seeds and membranes removed, coarsely chopped (see page 65 for roasting instructions)

2 scallions, coarsely chopped

1 cup (60 g) coarsely chopped cilantro leaves (about ½ bunch)

1 cup (67 g) coarsely chopped kale (about ½ bunch)

1 teaspoon salt

¼ cup (60 ml) water

2 tablespoons vegetable oil

2 tablespoons vegan margarine, such as Earth Balance

1½ cups (270 g) long grain white rice

2 cups (480 ml) vegetable broth

1 lime

1 In a blender, pulse the peppers, scallions, cilantro, kale, and salt with the water.

2 Heat the oil and margarine in a saucepan. When the margarine starts to liquefy, add the rice. Sauté, stirring occasionally, for about 3 minutes.

3 Add the blended ingredients to the pan and mix well. Simmer for 1 minute, then stir in vegetable broth.

4 Return the mixture to a simmer, then reduce the heat to low. Cover and cook until the liquid is completely absorbed and the rice is tender, about 14 minutes.

5 Remove the pan from the heat and let the rice sit, covered, for 5 minutes. Then uncover and squeeze lime juice over rice. Fluff up with a fork and enjoy!

TOLERANT BULGUR CHORIZO

Fills 16 tacos

MANY STUDENTS ON THE TACO CLEANSE are looking for new and exciting ways to fit wheat into their diet. We have devised a new method to replace the majority of protein in chorizo with complex carbohydrates. Wheat bulgur steps in to provide our favorite supernutrient, gluten, while maintaining the familiar heartiness. Try this with any breakfast taco or in the Tater Tot-Cho Taco (page 146).

2 cups (480 ml) water

1 cup (240 ml) tomato sauce

1 cup (240 ml) vegetable broth

¼ cup (60 ml) red wine vinegar

¼ cup (60 ml) soy sauce

1 tablespoon canola oil

2 garlic cloves

1 jalapeño, seeded

½ yellow onion, coarsely chopped

2 tablespoons ground cumin

2 tablespoons paprika

1 teaspoon salt

¼ teaspoon cayenne

2 cups (360 g) coarse wheat bulgur

1 Puree everything except the bulgur in a blender and set aside.

2 Lightly toast the bulgur in a large pot for 1 minute over medium-high heat, stirring constantly. Pour the contents of the blender into the pot and bring it to a boil over high heat. Reduce the heat to low and simmer covered for 30 minutes.

TIP If you are not sure if you can tolerate wheat, we recommend substituting TVP (texturized vegetable protein) and slowly increasing the amount of bulgur until you have overcome your prejudice against gluten.

QUICK CHIPOTLE BEANS FOR IMPERFECT PEOPLE

Makes 1½ cups (360 ml); fills 4 tacos

15 ounces (425 g) rinsed canned black or pinto beans (if using homemade, do not rinse)

1 tablespoon minced chipotle in adobo

2 garlic cloves, chopped

½ teaspoon salt

IF YOU HAVE TIME, HOMEMADE BEANS cooked to perfection are always going to be best. But the Taco Cleanse isn't about perfection; it's about eating tacos, and sometimes that means using shortcuts like canned beans and chipotles in adobo so that you can make a taco in less than five minutes.

1 Heat up the beans along with the minced chipotle, adobo sauce, garlic, and salt in a small saucepan. Warm through.

QUICK FRIJOLES CHARROS

Makes 2 cups (480 ml); fills 6 tacos

THIS RECIPE COMES TO US FROM TACO-MAKER
Nelly Ramirez, who blogs at
aneelee.wordpress.com. Nelly and her
whole family participated in a Medium-
level cleanse as part of one of our research
groups.

1 Warm the oil in a sauté pan over
medium heat. Add the tomatoes and
onions and sauté until the onions start to
soften, about 3 minutes. Add the beans and
their broth to the pan and warm through.
Add the spices, liquid smoke, and salt.
Cook until the sauce reduces.

> SUPER CLEANSE: You can replace the home-cooked
> beans with 2 cups (480 ml) rinsed canned beans and ¼
> cup (60 ml) vegetable broth.

1 tablespoon vegetable oil

1 small tomato, chopped

¼ medium sweet onion, diced

2 cups cooked pinto beans and their cooking
broth

½ teaspoon ground coriander

½ teaspoon paprika

¼ teaspoon black pepper

¼ teaspoon liquid smoke

¼ teaspoon salt

ION-CHARGED REFRIED BEANS

Fills 8 tacos

MAKING THESE BEANS WILL TAKE QUITE A WHILE, but it's really easy and completely worth it. They are the creamiest, most succulent beans you will ever eat. The best tacos are often the most simple, and these refried beans on a homemade tortilla with fresh Essential Pico de Gallo (page 115) can send you into a state of pure unadulterated bliss. If you spend some time before you start your cleanse making these beans, you will have fewer details to worry about during the Taco Cleanse, which will mean your bodymind will have more energy for cellular cleansing and rejuvenation. Enjoy with fried plantains, roasted potatoes, avocado, rajas, or just about any other component in the book.

1 Sort the beans. Pick out and discard any rocks and give the beans a rinse with cold water. Put them in a pot with 8 cups (2 L) water, the bay leaf, and the epazote and bring to a simmer. Simmer for 2 hours,

2 cups (386 g) dried pinto (or black) beans

1 bay leaf

1 tablespoon dried epazote or Mexican oregano, or an extra whole bay leaf

1 whole garlic bulb

¼ cup plus 1 tablespoon (75 ml) vegetable or canola oil (not olive oil)

2 teaspoons salt

One 10-ounce (283 g) can diced tomatoes with green chiles, such as Ro-Tel brand

1 onion, chopped

Unsweetened plant milk

stirring and adding more hot water as needed so that the water level stays above the beans and they don't get stuck on the bottom.

2 Meanwhile, to roast the garlic, heat up an oven or toaster oven to 400°F (200°C). Take the whole garlic bulb and carefully cut off the hairy top part. Form a cup of foil in your hand large enough to envelop the bulb, place the garlic in the foil, and pour 1 tablespoon of the oil over the cut part. Seal up the foil into a ball and roast for about 45 minutes. Let it cool slightly and then

(Recipe continues . . .)

ION-CHARGED
REFRIED BEANS,
OPPOSITE PAGE

REDEMPTION BEANS,
PAGE 84

push the garlic out of the papery skins. You can always roast garlic while you have something else savory in the oven.

3 Once the beans are soft, add the remaining ¼ cup oil, salt, tomatoes, and roasted garlic. Continue simmering for another hour at least. The longer they cook, the better they will taste. You can't overcook them because they are just going to get mashed up anyway.

4 Strain out excess water from the beans and remove the bay leaf. (Just a little water is fine, but if you still have a couple of inches over the beans, pour it out.) Brown the onion in a large cast-iron skillet and then add the bean mixture. After some of the water has evaporated, mash the beans with a potato masher. Add some plant milk and stir, adding more until you reach your desired consistency. Cook over low heat, stirring, for at least 5 minutes, adding more milk if necessary.

> SUPER CLEANSE: You can do the first step in a slow cooker if you have one.

REDEMPTION BEANS

Fills 16 tacos

THESE BEANS ARE INSPIRED by the island of Jamaica. You can use traditional green *gungo* peas or *gandules* (aka pigeon peas), or the common "red peas" more often known in the States as kidney beans. Turn on Bob Marley and sing a song of freedom as you make these beans. Serve on corn tortillas with fried plantains, Guacamole Viridis (page 126), and rice.

2 cups (390 g) dried gungo peas, pigeon peas, or red kidney beans

One 13-ounce (398 ml) can coconut milk

13 ounces (398 ml) water (one can full)

1 Scotch bonnet pepper or habanero, whole (diced if you want spicy)

2 bay leaves

1 teaspoon thyme

½ teaspoon ground allspice

3 garlic cloves, smashed

3 scallions, smashed

1 teaspoon salt

1 Soak the beans in water for at least 8 hours. Drain the water and add the beans to a pot along with the rest of the ingredients. Let simmer, covered, stirring occasionally, an hour or two until the beans are tender, depending on how old your beans are and what variety. Keep an eye on the water level and add more if you need to; don't let those beans burn! When they are done remove the bay leaf, the whole pepper, and the scallions.

> **SUPER CLEANSE:** Instead of cooking your own peas, just use canned peas. Rinse them and cook all the ingredients together in a pot for about 5 minutes, omitting the water.

VERACRUZ GIANT LIMAS

Fills 16 tacos

NOTHING MAKES YOUR SKIN GLOW like a diet high in olives! If you aren't an olive fan, we recommend seeking out the Castelvetrano variety from a high-end olive bar. You'll notice immediately that they are a brighter green than the other olive varieties. Like black olives, they aren't cured, so they have a more buttery, sweet taste. Of course, this recipe will work well with your standard green pimiento-stuffed olive, too, truly the food of the gods.

(Recipe continues . . .)

2 cups (390 g) dried giant lima beans (or regular lima beans)

3 bay leaves

7 garlic cloves

1 teaspoon salt

1 tablespoon cooking oil

1 white onion, chopped

Two 10-ounce (283 g) cans diced tomatoes with green chiles, such as Ro-Tel brand

1 teaspoon Mexican oregano

2 tablespoons sliced pickled jalapeños

½ cup (120 ml) sliced green olives

2 tablespoons pickling juice (from jalapeños if you like it hot, from the olives if you like it salty)

¼ cup (15 g) cilantro, chopped

Serve these beans on a corn tortilla with Mexican rice, Cashew Crema (page 127), extra olives, and cilantro.

1 Soak the lima beans overnight in plenty of water. Drain the beans and add them to a large pot. Add water to the pot until it is 2 inches higher than the beans. Add the bay leaves, 4 of the garlic cloves, and the salt. Simmer for about 45 minutes, or until the beans are just tender; if the beans are older this can take a while. Remove the bay leaves and any floating bean skins but don't drain, or if you do, reserve 1 cup (240 ml) of the bean cooking water.

2 When the beans are almost tender, heat a large saucepan and add the oil. Sauté the onion until softened, 3 to 5 minutes. Mince the remaining three garlic cloves, add to the saucepan, and sauté for 30 seconds, being careful not to burn the garlic. Add the beans, diced tomatoes, oregano, jalapeños, olives, and pickling juice. Simmer uncovered, stirring occasionally, for 20 minutes, or until most of the liquid is cooked off. If you start to run out of water before the beans are as tender as you like, add some of the reserved bean cooking water. If you start to run out of water before the beans are tender, add some of the bean cooking water.

HACK YOUR TACO CLEANSE: Make a giant batch of beans, drain the liquid, and keep in the freezer until you need them!

GALLO PINTO (COSTA RICAN RICE AND BEANS)

~~~~~~~~~~~~~~~~~~~~~~

Fills 16 tacos

THE NATIONAL DISH OF COSTA RICA will keep your belly full for hours, so you will have plenty of time for snorkeling with sea turtles or hanging out in a hammock contemplating your inner taco. This recipe is a bit involved, but you can make the beans and rice ahead of time (especially since the beans take time and the rice is better refrigerated overnight) and then cook up *Gallo Pinto* whenever the urge strikes. Eating it in the morning will leave you with a beautiful buzz throughout the day. Serve in a breakfast taco with the lime, Spirited Salsa Inglesa (page 116) or Salsa Lizano, tofu scramble, avocado, and fried plantains.

For the beans:

1 Soak the beans for at least 8 hours. If you live somewhere that is really hot (e.g., Texas in the summer), you should do this in the fridge.

Beans

1 cup (195 g) dried black beans

2 bay leaves

Rice

1 teaspoon vegetable broth powder, such as Vegeta, or a broth cube

2 cups (480 ml) water

1 cup (195 g) rice (any will work; I use basmati)

Gallo Pinto

1 teaspoon cumin seeds

1 teaspoon coriander seeds

2 ancho chile peppers, stemmed and seeded

1 tablespoon cooking oil

1 large onion, chopped

6 garlic cloves, chopped

⅓ cup (15 g) packed, chopped cilantro

1 lime

2 When the beans are done soaking, change the water (add about 7 cups, or 1,680 ml), add the bay leaves, and bring to a simmer. Simmer for around 90 minutes, but start checking the doneness of the beans at around 1 hour, because the timing will vary depending on how dry your beans are.

You can also do this step in a slow cooker. Whatever you do, make sure that you save some of the cooking water with the beans, because you will need it later.

For the rice:

1 Dissolve the broth powder in the 2 cups of water in a saucepan. Add the rice, bring to a simmer, then reduce the heat to almost off and cook for 35 to 60 minutes, depending on what kind of rice you are using. (Check your bag of rice for cooking times.)

For the gallo pinto:

1 Toast the cumin, coriander, and dried peppers in a dry skillet over medium heat until fragrant and then grind in either a spice grinder or mortar and pestle. Add enough oil to cover the bottom of the skillet and place it over medium heat. When the oil is hot, add the onion. Sauté for 5 minutes, or until the onion starts to turn translucent. Add the garlic and the spice mixture and

sauté another minute. Add a little more oil if you can't see any and turn the heat up. Add the rice and stir-fry for about a minute; break up any chunks, but don't smoosh the rice. Once all the rice has changed color, add the beans, starting with just 1 cup, until you have a pleasing ratio of rice to beans. Also add a splash of the bean cooking water. Gently mix. Once everything is heated through, adjust the spices, add the cilantro, and turn off the heat. To make the mold, press the gallo pinto into a small bowl, invert a plate on it, and then flip both over and lift up the bowl. Squeeze lime on top and serve with extra wedges.

> **SUPER CLEANSE:** If you are short on time while starting the Gallo Pinto or don't have whole cumin and coriander seeds, you can toast cumin and coriander powders and add them with the garlic. Anchos aren't spicy, but feel free to sub other fresh peppers like jalapeños or bell peppers—just add them at the same time as the garlic

BLUE CORN CHIP-CRUSTED TOFU

Makes 16 pieces; fills 8 tacos

ALERT: Are you getting enough of the color blue in your diet? Colors are so important to the way our bodies function, and since the ocean is blue, it's especially critical that our bodies get enough blue in. The thing is, it can be tough to get blue food into your everyday diet without making conscious choices to choose blue! We developed this recipe to help.

1 Preheat the oven to 400°F (200°C). Line a baking sheet with a silicone baking mat or parchment paper. Gather three bowls or containers with flat bottoms; Tupperware works great for this.

2 Slice the tofu into 8 slabs and pat them dry with a kitchen towel or press using your preferred method. Slice the slabs in half to make skinnier rectangles. Put the tofu in one of the bowls, add the lime juice

14 to 16 ounces (397 to 454 g) extra-firm tofu

Juice of 1 lime

1 tablespoon soy sauce

½ cup crushed blue corn tortilla chips (about 3 ounces/85 g)

½ teaspoon salt (if chips are unsalted)

½ teaspoon cumin

½ teaspoon paprika

½ teaspoon black pepper

¼ teaspoon cayenne

¼ teaspoon garlic powder

¼ teaspoon onion powder

2 tablespoons cornstarch

1 cup (240 ml) unsweetened soy milk

Cooking oil spray

and the soy sauce, and stir carefully to coat.

3 Put the crushed tortilla chips in a separate bowl and mix in the salt, if using, and spices. In another bowl, mix the cornstarch and soy milk with a fork.

(Recipe continues . . .)

"LIVING" CHIPOTLE SAUCE, PAGE 120

BLUE CORN CHIP-CRUSTED TOFU, OPPOSITE PAGE

4 Now it's time to form the breading assembly line! Put the seasoned tofu all the way over on your right. To the left, put the bowl of cornstarch and soy milk. To the left of that, put the bowl of crushed chips, and to the left of that put the baking sheet. With your right hand, take a rectangle of tofu, drop it in the cornstarch bowl, pull it out, and drop it into the corn chip bowl. Now, with your left hand, get as much chip coating on the tofu as you can, pull it out, and place it on the prepared baking sheet. Repeat with the rest of the tofu. Spray the whole lot with oil and bake for 20 minutes.

> SUPER CLEANSE: A great alternative to crusting your own tofu is to use Gardein Chipotle Lime Crispy Fingers. They won't be blue, though, so eat some blue corn chips on the side.

IRIDESCENT FRIED TOFU

Makes 16 pieces; fills 8 tacos

MEDITATE ON THE SOUND OF THE CRACKLING tofu as it fries in the oil. Say to yourself, "This taco will be enough. I am enough. Enough." Serve with crunchy vegetables and either a creamy or acidic sauce.

1 Slice the tofu into 8 slabs. Then slice each slab into a triangle. Gather three bowls or containers with flat bottoms;

14 to 16 ounces (397 to 454 g) firm tofu, drained and pressed

½ cup (60 g) all-purpose flour

3 teaspoons garlic powder

3 teaspoons paprika

½ teaspoon kelp powder, optional

3 teaspoons salt

1½ teaspoons black pepper

¼ cup (60 ml) Dijon mustard

¼ cup (60 ml) water

1 cup (60 g) panko or other vegan bread crumbs

Canola oil for frying

Tupperware works great for this. In one bowl, mix together the flour, 1 teaspoon garlic powder, 1 teaspoon paprika, ½ teaspoon kelp powder if using, 1 teaspoon salt, and ½ teaspoon of the pepper. In the second bowl, mix together the mustard and water. Mix the bread crumbs with the remaining 2 teaspoons garlic powder, 2 teaspoons paprika, 2 teaspoons salt, and 1 teaspoon pepper in the third bowl.

2 Heat ¼ inch (0.5 cm) of oil in a medium frying pan over medium heat.

3 While the pan heats, bread the tofu. Designate one hand wet and one hand dry. With your wet hand, grab a tofu triangle and drop it into the flour mixture. Using your dry hand, flip the tofu over so it gets covered in flour on all sides. Still using the dry hand, shake off any excess flour. Then place the tofu into the mustard mixture, being sure not to get your dry hand wet. Using your wet hand, flip the tofu so that it's coated on all sides. Remove the tofu with your wet hand and place it in the bread crumbs. Use your dry hand to flip and coat the tofu in bread crumbs. Set the coated tofu aside on a plate. Repeat with the rest of the tofu.

4 Fry the tofu in batches of 3 to 4 pieces for about 2 minutes on each side, or until light brown. Set aside on paper towels or a cooling rack to drain. In between batches of tofu, let the oil reheat for about 30 seconds.

VARIATION: If mustard is too twangy for your palate, replace it with the mayo from Rewarding Esquites (page 68) or a store-bought mayo, such as Vegenaise or Just Mayo.

> SUPER CLEANSE: Don't want to make kelp powder yourself by harvesting seaweed at the local beach? Find kelp powder in any health food store in the Asian section or at a Japanese market.

MIGHTY MIGAS

Fills 8 tacos

WHAT STARTED OUT as a way to use up leftover corn tortillas has become a staple of brunch tables. Migas tacos are transformational because they contain two superfoods: corn and flour tortillas. If you've been afflicted with collywobbles or gripe, try eating at least one migas taco a week. Because your homemade corn tortillas are probably too delicious to leave any leftovers, tortilla chips stand in here.

1 Heat the oil in a large sauté pan over medium-high heat. Sauté the onion and jalapeño for 2 minutes, or until the onion starts to soften. Crumble the tofu into the pan and sprinkle with the salt, cumin, and black pepper. Cook until the tofu is dry and browned on at least one side, about 10 minutes. Try not to stir too often as this prevents browning. Add the rest of the ingredients, including the cheese if you're using it, and stir thoroughly. Cook until the tomato softens and the liquid is completely absorbed. Serve in the flour tortillas.

1 tablespoon cooking oil

½ cup (70 g) chopped onion

1 jalapeño, sliced into rings

14 to 16 ounces (397 to 454 g) firm tofu, drained

1 teaspoon salt

½ teaspoon ground cumin

⅛ teaspoon black pepper

1 cup (37 g) crumbled tortilla chips

1 cup (170 g) seeded, chopped tomato

¼ cup (15 g) nutritional yeast

¼ cup (60 ml) unsweetened plant milk or water

½ cup (48 g) vegan cheddar, optional

8 Flour Tortillas (page 47) or store-bought

WAKE AND SHAKE SCRAMBLE

Fills 8 tacos

THE TOFU SCRAMBLE is arguably the defining element of a breakfast taco. This shake-and-bake version demands less supervision than an orthodox skillet scramble (see Mighty Migas on page 95 for our take on the stovetop scramble). Use the extra time to write in your taco journal (see page 26). Serve this scramble with Foundational Tempeh Bacon (page 105) and "Living" Chipotle Sauce (page 120).

Cooking oil

1 cup (60 g) nutritional yeast

1 teaspoon dried oregano

1 teaspoon ground cumin

½ teaspoon garlic powder

½ teaspoon onion powder

½ teaspoon paprika

½ teaspoon black pepper

½ teaspoon salt

14 to 16 ounces (397 to 454 g) firm tofu, drained and pressed

1 Preheat the oven to 350°F (175°C). Oil a baking sheet.

2 Add the nutritional yeast, spices, and salt to a paper lunch bag. Fold the top of the bag and shake until the ingredients are combined. Tear the tofu into bite-size pieces. Place a handful of the tofu pieces into the seasoning bag, fold the top, and shake until evenly coated. Reach into the bag and sift the golden nuggets of tofu out of the seasoning mixture with your fingers. Place the nuggets in a single layer on the prepared baking sheet. Repeat with the rest of the tofu. Bake for 30 minutes, flipping the tofu over once.

TEQUILA SAUSAGE,
PAGE 104

SOY CURL FAJITAS,
OPPOSITE PAGE

SOY CURL FAJITAS

Fills 6 tacos

WE LOVE SOY CURLS because they are so easy to make and have a great texture. They are essentially just dried soybeans, so if you are one of those people who endlessly worries about processed food . . . stop! Relax and eat a taco. Serve these on a tortilla with homemade Guacamole Viridis (page 126) or plant-based sour cream and scallions or sliced almonds for some crunch.

1 Soak the Soy Curls in the warm vegetable broth for 5 minutes. Squeeze out as much of the broth as you can. Set the soy curls aside. The leftover broth can be reserved for another use.

2 Heat up a cast-iron skillet over medium-high heat and then add the oil. When the oil is shimmering, toss in the peppers and onion. After about 5 minutes, when they are getting browned, add the garlic, and after it sizzles for 30 seconds, add the Soy Curls and other ingredients. Cook until the Soy Curls are browned.

2 cups (50 g) Soy Curls

2 cups (240 ml) vegetable broth, warmed

¼ cup (60 ml) olive oil

1 red bell pepper, cut in strips

1 orange bell pepper, cut in strips

1 white onion, cut in half moons

4 garlic cloves, chopped

2 tablespoons aji amarillo pepper sauce (see Super Cleanse)

1 tablespoon habanero hot sauce, such as Yellowbird Sauce (see Super Cleanse)

1 teaspoon cumin

2 tablespoons soy sauce

2 teaspoons fajita seasoning mix

> **SUPER CLEANSE:** This recipe calls for two of our favorite pepper-based sauces, but of course you can always substitute your favorite hot sauce and add any of your favorite minced peppers in place of the aji amarillo.

ENLIGHTENED SOY CURLS AL PASTOR

Fills 6 tacos

YOU ARE GOING TO LOVE THIS plant-based version of authentic al pastor tacos. Serve on homemade corn tortillas topped with minced onions, cilantro, and lime juice.

1 Simmer the Soy Curls, water, broth powder, chiles, and epazote for 10 minutes in a medium saucepan. With a spoon, pick the dried peppers out and set aside, leaving the Soy Curls and broth in the pan to cool.

2 When cool enough to handle, remove the stems and seeds from the chiles. In a blender, combine the chiles with all of the marinade ingredients. Add the blended marinade to the saucepan with the Soy Curls. Refrigerate 1 hour.

3 Heat up a cast-iron skillet and add the oil. Sauté the onion and garlic for a couple of minutes and then add the Soy Curls with the marinade and the remaining pineapple. Sauté until the Soy Curls start to brown, about 15 minutes. Serve on the corn tortillas with the minced onion, cilantro, and lime juice to taste.

2½ cups (63 g) Soy Curls
3 cups (720 ml) water
1 packet vegetable broth powder, such as Goya Ham Flavored Concentrate
2 ancho chiles
1 guajillo chile
1 tablespoon epazote

Marinade

½ cup (120 ml) water
¼ cup (60 ml) lime juice
2 chipotles in adobo, plus 2 teaspoons of the adobo sauce
¼ cup (41 g) diced pineapple
1 teaspoon sugar or agave nectar
1 teaspoon achiote paste
1 teaspoon oregano (preferably Mexican)
1 teaspoon ground cumin
1 teaspoon salt

Sauté

2 tablespoons cooking oil
1 small white onion, chopped
4 garlic cloves, chopped
¼ cup (41 g) diced pineapple

6 Corn Tortillas (page 49) or store-bought
Minced white onion
Minced cilantro
Lime juice

SINCERE SRIRACHA–AGAVE TENDERS

Fills 8 tacos

THESE SRIRACHA-AGAVE TENDERS begin with a hummus base and bring in gluten flour and panko bread crumbs for structure. The sriracha and agave are wonderful partners who embrace each other wholeheartedly. A quick pan-fry after baking will brown and crisp the tenders handsomely. The tenders are best accompanied by Naturalistic Corn Gravy (page 132) and High-Vibration Kale Chips (page 134).

1 Preheat the oven to 375°F (190°C). Oil a baking sheet.

2 Stir together the hummus, panko, soy sauce, agave nectar, sriracha, and thyme in a large bowl. Incorporate the vital wheat gluten ¼ cup at a time. Knead the ingredients in the bowl for 3 minutes to develop the gluten. Flatten the dough into a rectangle ¼ inch (0.5 cm) thick, then cut into 1 x 4-inch (2.5 x 10 cm) strips. Arrange

Cooking oil

2 cups (480 ml/450 g) Limitless Hummus (page 129) or store-bought

¾ cup (45 g) panko bread crumbs

¼ cup (60 ml) soy sauce

2 tablespoons agave nectar

3 tablespoons sriracha hot sauce

2 teaspoons dried thyme

1 cup (130 g) vital wheat gluten

the strips in a single layer on the baking sheet. Bake for 30 minutes, flipping the strips once halfway through.

TIP Did you know that before sriracha gained popularity, there were many different styles of hot sauce? Expand your palate and experiment with other exciting varieties. For example, replace the sriracha with Louisiana hot sauce for a Buffalo-style flavor.

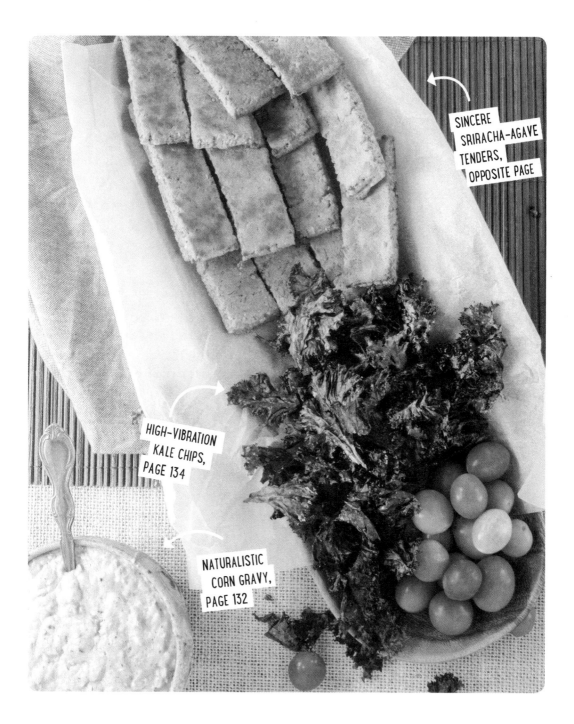

SINCERE SRIRACHA-AGAVE TENDERS, OPPOSITE PAGE

HIGH-VIBRATION KALE CHIPS, PAGE 134

NATURALISTIC CORN GRAVY, PAGE 132

TEQUILA SAUSAGE

Makes 4 sausages; fills 8 tacos

MAKING VEGAN SAUSAGE IS ALWAYS GLADDENING, and since this recipe includes tequila, you will have an easy time getting your Supplements in. You can take some shots while they steam and it will be even more fun! Just don't burn yourself. This sausage also includes almond meal (aka almond flour), a superbonus. Bob's Red Mill makes a prepackaged version, but you can also just blend or food-process almonds into a powder. American mystic Edgar Cayce has reported on almonds' special healing properties: "And know, if ye would take each day, through thy experience, two almonds, ye will never have skin blemishes, ye will never be tempted even in body toward cancer or towards those things that make blemishes in the body-forces themselves."

Slice the finished sausages in half, sauté with onion and kale or broccoli, and then top with Fried Plantains (page 67) and Essential Pico de Gallo (page 115).

Dry ingredients

7 garlic cloves, minced

2 teaspoons minced fresh sage

1 heaping teaspoon fennel seeds, crushed

¼ teaspoon cayenne

1 heaping teaspoon salt

1¼ cups (163 g) vital wheat gluten

¼ cup (23 g) almond meal

1 teaspoon red pepper flakes

Wet ingredients

½ cup (130 g) Ion-Charged Refried Beans (page 82) or store-bought refried pinto beans (or mashed cooked pintos)

⅔ cup (160 ml) vegetable broth

⅓ cup (80 ml) tequila

1 tablespoon olive oil

1 Prepare a steaming apparatus (for example, a pot of water with a bamboo or metal steamer sitting on top).

2 Mix together the dry ingredients in one bowl and the wet ingredients in another. After everything is well incorporated, add the wet ingredients to the dry and knead for a minute or two.

3 Lay a piece of foil on the counter. Place ½ cup (120 ml) of the mixture in the center of the bottom third of the foil. Roll up into a link and then tie off each end, like a Tootsie Roll. Repeat with the rest of the mixture. Steam the links for 30 minutes and then refrigerate.

4 Before eating, remove from the foil and sauté. Tequila Sausages can be stored in their foil for about two weeks in the fridge or two months in the freezer.

> **SUPER CLEANSE:** Field Roast makes a great alternative sausage, although they don't yet do a tequila version.

FOUNDATIONAL TEMPEH BACON

Fills 6 tacos

WHO SAYS BACON HAS TO COME IN STRIPS?
These tempeh bacon cubes are easier to make and easier to eat in a taco than the traditional strips. Tempeh bacon goes great with other breakfast ingredients in a breakfast taco. Try it with hash browns and tofu scramble.

1 Heat the oil in a large sauté pan over medium heat. Add the tempeh cubes and cook, stirring occasionally, for about 8 minutes, or until a few sides of each cube are brown and crispy.

(Recipe continues . . .)

2 tablespoons canola oil

8 ounces (227 g) tempeh, in ¼-inch (0.5 cm) cubes

1 teaspoon brown sugar

½ teaspoon chipotle powder

¼ teaspoon kosher salt

¼ teaspoon coarsely ground black pepper

2 tablespoons water

2 tablespoons tamari or low-sodium soy sauce

1 tablespoon apple cider vinegar

1 tablespoon maple syrup

1 teaspoon liquid smoke

2 While the tempeh cooks, combine the rest of the ingredients and set aside.

3 When the tempeh is ready, add the liquid mixture and cook for 5 minutes, or until the liquid is thickened and mostly absorbed.

TIP To liberate the tempeh from its plastic wrapping, cut straight through the whole package with a knife, then squeeze out both halves.

SUPER CLEANSE: There are several brands of bacon alternatives available at many grocery stores. Lightlife makes a fakin' bacon that's very similar to this recipe. If you prefer a seitan version, seek out the Upton's Naturals brand or the Hickory and Sage Smoked Seitan Bacon from Sweet Earth.

THERAPEUTIC TEMPEH PICADILLO

Fills 8 tacos

COOKING *PICADILLO* IS ALCHEMY. Seemingly discordant base ingredients combine in a skillet to form the taco equivalent of gold. Olives and raisins swirl together in a stew of reliable components to create a depth of flavor greater than the sum of its parts. Let the savory broth soak into Arroz Verde (see page 77) on a flour tortilla and ponder its complexity.

1 vegetable bouillon cube

½ cup (120 ml) hot water

1 tablespoon olive oil

1 yellow onion, diced

16 ounces (454 g) tempeh

2 garlic cloves, minced

1 teaspoon dried oregano

1 teaspoon ground cumin

¼ teaspoon black pepper

¼ teaspoon salt

One 15-ounce (444 ml) can diced tomatoes

⅓ cup (80 ml) red wine

⅓ cup (54 g) raisins

⅓ cup (74 g) pimiento-stuffed olives, drained and chopped

2 tablespoons olive brine

1. In a small bowl, dissolve the bouillon cube in the hot water and set aside.

2. In a large skillet, heat the oil over medium heat. Add the onion and sauté for 5 minutes, or until translucent. Crumble the tempeh by hand into the skillet and cook for 5 minutes, stirring occasionally. Add the garlic and stir. Then add the oregano, cumin, pepper, and salt. Allow the spices to toast in the skillet for 30 seconds. Add the previously prepared bouillon and the tomatoes and red wine to the skillet. Deglaze the skillet by scraping the bottom with a spatula. Bring the mixture to a steady simmer. Fold in the raisins, olives, and brine. Reduce the heat and simmer uncovered for 20 minutes.

TIP This recipe calls for ⅓ cup of red wine, leaving the remainder of the bottle to drink while you finish cooking.

"Eighty percent of success is eating tacos."
—WOODY ALLEN

REVITALIZING TACO SEITAN

Fills 16 tacos

VITAL WHEAT GLUTEN is made from wheat flour that has been rinsed until the starches have washed away and only the vitality remains. You should be able to feel the revitalizing effects immediately when this superfood is included in your taco. Finely chop it in a food processor for classic taco crumbles or fry as we do for Artisan Seitan Strips (see page 112).

1 Preheat the oven to 350°F (175°C). Oil an 8 x 8-inch (20 x 20 cm) cake pan.

2 Combine the vital wheat gluten and spices in a large bowl and whisk thoroughly. In a second bowl, stir together the broth, oil, and soy sauce. Pour the liquid mixture into the dry mixture and knead by hand until just combined. Unlike many seitan recipes, the gluten does not need to be developed, and the dough will be much softer. Flatten the dough into the prepared pan and cover with aluminum foil. Bake for 60 minutes. Flip the seitan at the 30-minute mark and cover again with foil.

2 cups (260 g) vital wheat gluten

1 teaspoon dried oregano

1 teaspoon garlic powder

1 teaspoon ground cumin

1 teaspoon onion powder

1 teaspoon paprika

2 cups (480 ml) vegetable broth

2 tablespoons olive oil

2 tablespoons soy sauce

SUPER CLEANSE: There is an abundance of vegan ground beef available in the grocery store. If you don't have time to make seitan, buy some crumbles. Brown the crumbles with a splash of oil in a skillet and add a heaping spoonful of chili powder.

COMFORTING SEITAN GUISADA

Fills 8 tacos

GUISADA IS A MILD STEW that can be used as a natural stress reducer. Add it to your taco to settle an excited mind. On a cold day, invite the guisada to hug your aura. It works well in a taco once the gravy has thickened, especially when combined with steamed rice.

½ batch Revitalizing Taco Seitan (page 109) or 16 ounces (454 g) store-bought

3 tablespoons canola oil

1 green bell pepper, diced

1 onion, diced

3 tablespoons all-purpose flour

1 teaspoon cumin

1 teaspoon black pepper

½ teaspoon salt

2 cups (480 ml) vegetable broth

1 Chop the seitan into bite-size pieces and set aside.

2 Heat the oil over medium-high heat in a large pot and sauté the bell pepper and onion for about 5 minutes, until softened. Add the flour and stir for a minute until you can smell it lightly toasting. Add the seitan, spices, salt, and broth. Bring it to a boil, then simmer over low heat for 15 minutes. The gravy will thicken slightly once removed from the heat.

SUPER CLEANSE: If seitan is not on hand, it can be easily replaced with Soy Curls or white kidney beans.

ARTISAN SEITAN STRIPS

Fills 8 tacos

TO BATTER THE STRIPS, this seitan recipe uses the time-honored paper bag technique, which still works well in modern times. Mastering this craft is personally rewarding and honors tradition. Visualize the strips inside the bag to ensure even seasoning. These strips and our Superpure Country Gravy (page 131) are a natural pair when food-combining. Enveloping both in a flour tortilla is your opportunity to demonstrate gluten tolerance.

1 In a shallow bowl, whisk together the soy milk and vinegar. In a paper bag, combine the flour, baking powder, salt, and spices.

2 Heat the oil over medium-high heat in a large skillet while preparing the seitan. Slice the seitan into ¼-inch (0.5 cm) thick strips. For the breading, dip the seitan strips into the soy milk mixture. Then, in

1 cup (240 ml) unsweetened soy milk

½ teaspoon apple cider vinegar

1 cup (120 g) all-purpose flour

1 tablespoon baking powder

1 teaspoon salt

1 teaspoon dried thyme

1 teaspoon black pepper

½ teaspoon garlic powder

½ teaspoon onion powder

½ teaspoon paprika

½ cup (120 ml) canola oil

½ batch Revitalizing Taco Seitan (page 109) or 16 ounces (454 g) store-bought

small batches, move them to the paper bag, fold the top, and shake until evenly coated.

3 Remove the strips from the bag and fry the breaded strips in the heated skillet for 3 minutes on each side. Take care not to crowd the skillet as it will reduce the temperature of the oil. Remove the fried seitan strips from the skillet and rest them on a clean paper bag to absorb excess oil.

CONDIMENTS

Condiments are the finishing element of a taco and the key to uncovering your taco personality. Focus a microscope on your inner bodymind. Where are you in your taco journey? Are you spicy? Acidic? Or bland?

Adjust your levels based on these observations. Restore your vigor with vinegar-based sauces. Cool overheated passion with Jalapeño Ranch or Cashew Crema. Fire up zeal with Salsa Inglesa. Soothe a broken heart or a burnt tongue with Salsa Verde.

It's easy to get caught up in where you think you should be. Don't jump into habanero salsa because of peer pressure. Your needs will change frequently, and so should your condiments. The salsa that tastes too spicy today may be just right tomorrow.

Perform this self-evaluation frequently throughout your Taco Cleanse. Ask yourself, what does this taco need? What do I need? Remember, the Taco Cleanse isn't about masochistic heat tolerance; it's about transforming yourself at the molecular level.

And remember, giving the gift of salsa elevates levels in a corresponding fashion. See our recipes for homemade salsa on pages 114–120 for ideas. Be sure to follow directions to safely jar your salsa for storage, or just keep the jars refrigerated if your salsa will be eaten right away. Your friends and family will be so delighted to open their salsa presents!

SALSA ROJA

Makes about 4 cups (960 mL)

COOKED TOMATOES HAVE TONS OF LYCOPENE. According to holistic guru Dr. Weil, "Lycopene is also found in cell membranes and plays an important role in maintaining the cell's integrity when it is under assault by toxins." This salsa will provide you with the tools you need to fight the good fight before you go "insane in the membrane."

Serve warm with chips and margaritas, atop breakfast tacos and tofu scramble, or with Ion-Charged Refried Beans (page 82) and avocado on a fresh Corn Tortilla (page 49). This salsa will keep in a jar in the refrigerator for a few weeks.

1 Turn on the broiler in the oven after moving the rack to the highest level. Put the tomatoes, jalapeños, onion, and garlic cloves on a baking sheet and slide under the broiler. Check every 2 minutes and rotate once the vegetables begin to blister and turn black. Repeat this process until the vegetables are about 25 percent black. You may remove the smaller vegetables, like the

8 roma tomatoes, cores removed

2 jalapeños, cut in half (seeded if you don't want it spicy)

1 large white onion, cut in half

3 garlic cloves

¼ cup (15 g) cilantro

1 tablespoon lime juice

1 teaspoon salt

1 teaspoon ancho chile powder or other powdered pepper

¼ teaspoon sugar

garlic, first, since they will blacken sooner. Transfer to a food processor and pulse along with the remaining ingredients until a chunky sauce is created.

TIP To make salsa verde, substitute an equal amount of tomatillos—paper coverings and sticky substance removed—for the tomatoes.

SUPER CLEANSE: Buy salsa from the store. Just make sure to check that it's made in the Southwest or Mexico. You don't want your friends to look at it and say, "This stuff's made in New York City?!"

ESSENTIAL PICO DE GALLO

Makes 2 cups (480 ml)

THIS SALSA IS THE CROWN OF SO MANY TACOS.
Eating it daily, one is able to enter a state of true beingness. It is most delicious at the height of summer when tomatoes are in their full glory. But, since you salt the tomatoes and put them in the fridge for a bit, and you need firm tomatoes, boring winter tomatoes will work fine, too. The more finely you chop the main ingredients, the better.

1 Dice the tomatoes first, sprinkle them with salt, and leave in a colander while you chop the remaining ingredients. Toss the remaining ingredients together in a large bowl and then add the tomatoes. If you can, refrigerate for an hour before serving to let the flavors meld. This is best served the same day.

1 pound (454 g) firm tomatoes such as plum or roma, about 8 plum tomatoes

½ teaspoon salt

¼ cup (15 g) packed, finely chopped cilantro

½ jalapeño, seeded and finely chopped

1 tablespoon lime juice

½ small white onion, finely chopped, about ¼ cup (40 g)

TIP If you can't stand all that fine chopping, then you can pulse the ingredients in a food processor. First pulse the seeded jalapeño and cilantro. Next, quarter the onion and pulse until it's chopped. Then add the tomato, lime, and salt. You will only need to pulse a few times once you add the tomato; you don't want to end up with tomato juice!

SPIRITED SALSA INGLESA

Makes 1 cup (240 ml)

THIS SAVORY BROWN SAUCE is an interpretation of Salsa Lizano, a Costa Rican condiment similar to Worcestershire sauce. It's tart and goes especially well with tofu scrambles and black beans. Using Salsa Inglesa provides the same curative effects as drinking vinegar, without the bracing aftershock. Store it in a condiment bottle and let the stratosphere of flavors mellow out in the fridge for a while. This is the perfect companion for Gallo Pinto (page 88).

1 guajillo pepper, stemmed and seeded
1 cup (240 ml) vegetable broth
½ yellow onion, diced
1 small carrot, diced
1 celery stalk, diced
¼ cup (60 ml) lemon juice
½ cup (120 ml) apple cider vinegar
¼ cup (60 ml) soy sauce
¼ cup (60 ml) water
2 garlic cloves
1 tablespoon agave nectar
1 tablespoon molasses
1 teaspoon tamarind pulp
½ teaspoon ground mustard seed
¼ teaspoon black pepper
¼ teaspoon ground allspice
2 tablespoons cornstarch

1 Simmer the guajillo pepper in the broth in a medium saucepan for 5 minutes, or until soft. Pour both the hydrated pepper and the broth into a blender. In the saucepan, sauté the onion, carrot, and celery over medium-high heat until softened and slightly browned. Add the sautéed veggies and the remaining ingredients except the cornstarch to the blender. Puree until smooth.

2 Use a sieve to strain the liquids back into the saucepan. Discard any solids. Bring the strained liquid to a gentle boil. Sprinkle the cornstarch into the liquid while whisking constantly to prevent lumps. Once the cornstarch thickens the sauce, remove from the heat and let cool. Store the sauce in a condiment bottle and keep refrigerated for up to several weeks.

FRUITY SALSA

Makes about 1 cup (240 ml)

THE GOVERNMENT SAYS that a quarter of your plate should be filled with fruit, so load up on fruity salsa. Big Brother is always watching. The optional citrus juice is useful if you're using fruit that browns, such as apples. This formula works great with lots of fruits, so get creative.

1 Combine the ingredients and refrigerate for up to three days depending on the fruit you use.

1 cup (240 ml) chopped pineapple, mango, apple, or cucumber

2 tablespoons minced red onion

2 tablespoons chopped cilantro

1 jalapeño, seeded and minced

Pinch of salt

Squeeze of lemon or lime juice, optional

CREAMY JALAPEÑO SALSA

Makes about 1 cup (240 ml)

1 bulb garlic

6 tablespoons canola oil, or any other neutral oil, plus more for roasting garlic

½ pound (237 g) jalapeños, or around 5 to 7 peppers

⅛ teaspoon ground cumin

Pinch of salt

THIS SAUCE HAS BEEN HANDED DOWN through the ages from one taco scientist to another. It's not for spice wimps. Wise cleansers won't waste their good olive oil on this recipe since the jalapeños will overwhelm any subtle flavors. Use this salsa on any taco that needs a bit of creamy heat.

1 Heat the oven to 400°F (200°C) and line a baking sheet with tinfoil. Cut off the stem end of the garlic bulb just enough to let the bulb rest flat. Cut off the very top of the root end of the bulb, exposing the tops of the garlic cloves. Place the garlic bulb on the baking sheet and drizzle with a tiny bit of oil. Add the jalapeños to the baking sheet and bake for 45 minutes to an hour, turning once, until the jalapeño skins are wrinkly and beginning to blacken.

2 Remove the garlic bulb and set aside. Fold the edges of the aluminum foil over the jalapeños, making an airtight packet. The steam trapped in the packet will help loosen the skins. Once the jalapeños are cool enough to touch, remove the stems, skins, and seeds. Rinsing the peppers under water will help remove all the seeds. If you like extra spicy food, leave the seeds.

3 Once the garlic bulb is cool enough to touch, squeeze out the individual garlic cloves.

4 In a blender, puree the prepared jalapeños, 3 to 4 garlic cloves, and the rest of the ingredients until creamy and uniform in color.

5 Keep for up to two weeks in the refrigerator. Use sparingly; it's hot!

"LIVING" CHIPOTLE SAUCE

Makes 1½ cups (360 ml)

IN THE NORTHERNMOST REACHES OF AUSTIN exists a vegan taco truck that serves a magical orange elixir. An expedition to this fabled parking lot is not always feasible for distant Austinites, compelling one taco alchemist to attempt re-creating the potion. While not an exact mimic, it provides similar cleansing properties. This sauce is pure wizardry, and your magic wand is the immersion blender. We recommend it with Wake and Shake Scramble (page 96) and Foundational Tempeh Bacon (page 105).

1 With an immersion blend, pulverize the chipotles in a quart-size, wide-mouth mason jar. While continuing to blend the chipotles, slowly drizzle the oil into the jar. Practice patience in this moment. A thin,

One 7.5-ounce (212 g) can chipotles in adobo
1 cup (240 ml) canola oil
Juice of 2 limes
½ teaspoon garlic powder
½ teaspoon onion powder
¼ teaspoon salt

steady stream of oil is key to the success of this recipe. The color of the adobo sauce will dramatically shift to bright orange when performed correctly. Add the lime juice, garlic powder, onion powder, and salt to the jar and blend for a moment. Transfer the sauce to a condiment bottle and keep refrigerated for up to a few weeks.

CILANTRO-AVOCADO TRANQUILITY SAUCE

Makes about 2½ cups (600 ml)

1 avocado

3 tablespoons vegan yogurt

½ teaspoon salt

Juice of one lime

½ cup (25 g) cilantro

¼ cup (120 ml) water

⅛ teaspoon white pepper

THIS SAUCE IS GREAT for cooling down a spicy filling, and it also goes well with fried potatoes. To cool the mind, avoid negative, critical thoughts and consider a soothing meditation. For example, chant "Every taco I eat is the perfect taco for me" seventeen times.

1 Blend all of the ingredients on high speed in a blender until combined. Transfer the sauce to a condiment bottle and keep refrigerated for up to three days.

SUPER CLEANSE: We prefer the So Delicious brand of plain yogurt, but other varieties of soy, almond, or coconut yogurt will work as well. Make sure it is unsweetened and contains no vanilla flavoring. Research at the University of California, Davis, showed that eating live-culture yogurt was associated with higher-than-average levels of gamma interferon. Contrary to the message of popular TV commercials, yogurt can be enjoyed by men as well.

SOOTHING JALAPEÑO RANCH

Makes 2 cups (480 ml)

WHILE ON THE TACO CLEANSE, you may experience flashes of insight concerning secret sauces. Use this knowledge to experiment with creating restaurant favorites in your personal kitchen laboratory. This tribute to a local Tex-Mex joint's jalapeño ranch dip came in a lucid dream of a founding taco scientist.

¾ cup (180 ml) soy milk
1 tablespoon lemon juice
1 cup (240 ml) canola oil
1 jalapeño, seeded
1 scallion
½ cup (25 g) cilantro
1 teaspoon garlic powder
1 teaspoon onion powder
½ teaspoon dried dill
½ teaspoon salt

1 Pour the soy milk and lemon juice into a quart-size, wide-mouth mason jar. Insert an immersion blender into the jar and blend at its highest setting. While blending the contents of the jar, drizzle the oil into the jar very slowly in a thin stream. Make sure the contents have thickened before continuing. Add the remaining ingredients and puree until smooth. Transfer the sauce to a condiment bottle and keep refrigerated for up to three days.

TARTAR SAUCE

Makes 1 cup (240 ml)

PICKLING CONCENTRATES THE LIFE FORCES OF VEGETABLES. It also works for humans if you substitute tequila for vinegar. Since this recipe contains two pickled foods, it's pretty much the healthiest thing you'll ever eat.

Serve with Blue Corn Chip–Crusted Tofu (page 90), Iridescent Fried Tofu (page 92), or other fried foods.

1 cup (240 ml) vegan mayo from Rewarding Esquites (page 68) or store-bought
2 tablespoons diced dill pickle
1 tablespoon diced capers

1 Stir together all ingredients. Keep refrigerated for up to three days.

BRIGHT-EYED BUFFALO SAUCE

Makes ½ cup (120 ml)

THIS IS THE PERFECT SAUCE FOR TACOS that need a spicy kick in the face and a soft pillow to land on. It's perfect with our Zucchini Fritters (page 66).

¼ cup (60 ml) vegan mayo from Rewarding Esquites (page 68) or store-bought
1 tablespoon nutritional yeast
1 tablespoon Frank's RedHot sauce
¼ teaspoon salt
2 tablespoons plant milk

1 Stir everything together in a small bowl, perhaps with a fork. Keep refrigerated for up to three days.

CASHEW CREMA

Makes about 1 cup (240 mL)

1 cup (120g) raw cashews, soaked
2 tablespoons plain kombucha

CREMA IS A BIT LIKE SOUR CREAM, but it's a little more . . . creamy. We use a bit of kombucha as a fermenting agent because what kind of cleanse would this be without kombucha? The ancient Chinese called this fermented tea the "Immortal Health Elixir," for good reason—did you know it has been reported to reduce gray hair? Original flavor will work best; just make sure it's raw because the microorganisms need to be alive to ferment the crema. Soak the cashews for about 24 hours for maximum creaminess; if you can't soak them that long you may need to add some water while blending.

1 In a blender, blend all the ingredients 2 to 5 minutes, until creamy. Start on a lower speed and move up to a higher speed as the mixture comes together. Pour the mix in a glass bowl and cover with a kitchen towel and let it ferment for about 48 hours at room temperature. After this, you can store it in the fridge and use for a few weeks.

SUPER CLEANSE: If this recipe seems like it takes a long time to make, what with the soaking and fermenting, try Tofutti Sour Supreme instead.

BREAKTHROUGH BBQ SAUCE

Makes 3 cups (720 mL)

THIS BEAUTIFUL BBQ SAUCE has a deep red color that calls in the force of the root chakra. Can you hear it? It's telling you to follow your most basic instincts, like slathering BBQ sauce on everything.

One 24-ounce (710 ml) can tomato sauce
¼ cup (60 ml) prepared brown mustard
¼ cup (53 g) white sugar
3 tablespoons molasses
1 tablespoon paprika
2 teaspoons garlic powder
2 teaspoons onion powder
1 teaspoon liquid smoke
1 teaspoon salt
½ teaspoon ground allspice

1 Combine all the BBQ sauce ingredients in a medium saucepan. Bring the mixture to a boil. Reduce heat to low and simmer, uncovered, for at least 15 minutes, whisking occasionally. Keep refrigerated for up to two weeks.

GUACAMOLE VIRIDIS

Serves 4

2 avocados
½ teaspoon salt
Juice from ½ lime

TRADITIONALLY, when guacamole is served as a dip with chips, it is mixed with all sorts of ingredients, maybe even orange juice. When serving it on tacos, we keep it super simple to add a cooling element to your taco that doesn't contrast with the other flavors. Adding guacamole to your tacos will shake any patterns of disharmony that you've developed and can prevent against Irumodic Syndrome.

1 Peel and pit the avocados and mash with a potato masher or fork. Stir in the salt and lime, adjusting to taste. Try with any taco combination you like. Guacamole is like the color black; it goes with everything.

LIMITLESS HUMMUS

Makes 2 cups (480 ml)

AS EVERY VEGETARIAN KNOWS WELL, hummus is the ubiquitous chickpea spread available in every crudité platter and falafel sandwich. Rather than dismiss this omnipresent paste, we embrace its availability. Hummus is there for us wherever a dry taco needs a creamy savior. While it's true that hummus can host myriad flavors, this version remains neutral in order to support a wide range of tacos. We also call upon Limitless Hummus as the foundation of Sincere Sriracha-Agave Tenders (page 102), transforming it from a mere dip into a full-fledged taco filling.

Two 15.5-ounce (439 g) cans chickpeas, drained and rinsed
2 garlic cloves
1 teaspoon salt
2 tablespoons lemon juice
2 tablespoons tahini
2 tablespoons olive oil
¼ cup (60 ml) water

1 In a food processor, puree all the ingredients except for the water until smooth. Scrape down the sides of the processor with a rubber spatula if needed. Slowly drizzle the water into the running food processor until your desired consistency is reached.

MINIMALIST NACHO CHEESE

Makes 3 cups (710 ml)

SOMETIMES THE BEST CHEESE SAUCE is the one you can make the fastest. Our taco scientists have engineered the Minimalist Nacho Cheese for instant gratification. It is intelligently designed with shelf-stable ingredients from a rudimentary taco cellar.

1 Begin the cheesy sauce by adding the oil and flour to a medium saucepan over medium heat. Whisk constantly for 3 minutes, or until the flour is lightly toasted. Add the cumin, garlic powder, onion powder, paprika, and salt while continuing to whisk for another minute. Pour the soy milk into the pan and increase the heat until the sauce thickens. Immediately lower the heat to a simmer. Whisk in the nutritional yeast, jalapeños, brine if using, and lemon juice. Keep refrigerated for up to three days.

¼ cup (60 ml) olive oil

3 tablespoons all-purpose flour

2 teaspoons ground cumin

1 teaspoon garlic powder

1 teaspoon onion powder

1 teaspoon paprika

1 teaspoon salt

2 cups (480 ml) unsweetened soy milk

½ cup (30 g) nutritional yeast

¼ cup (40 g) pickled jalapeño slices, drained and chopped

2 tablespoons pickled jalapeño brine, optional

2 tablespoons lemon juice

ELEVATED NACHO CHEESE

Makes 3½ cups (830 ml)

THERE WILL INHERENTLY BE OCCASIONS on your taco journey when a more sophisticated nacho sauce is suitable. The Elevated Nacho Cheese ingredients have been curated by our local taco artisans to reveal exceptional creaminess and depth.

1 In a medium saucepan, heat the oil over medium-high heat. Sauté the potato and cashews in the pan for 1 minute, or until the cashews are lightly toasted. Add the spices and salt. Continue to sauté for 1 more minute. Add the soy milk, water, lemon juice, and brine if using. Bring to a boil and then simmer over low heat for 10 minutes, or until the potato is tender.

2 Relocate the contents of the saucepan to a blender. Blend until smooth. Hold the lid ajar to prevent steam from building up in the blender. Fold the jalapeños into the cheesy sauce. Keep refrigerated for up to three days.

¼ cup (60 ml) olive oil
½ small russet potato, peeled and diced
1 cup unsalted raw cashews
2 teaspoons ground cumin
1 teaspoon garlic powder
1 teaspoon onion powder
1 teaspoon paprika
1 teaspoon salt
2 cups (480 ml) unsweetened soy milk
½ cup (120 ml) water
2 tablespoons lemon juice
2 tablespoons pickled jalapeño brine, optional
¼ cup (40 g) pickled jalapeño slices, drained and chopped

TIP Clean your blender easily by filling it halfway with soapy water and turning it on.

SUPERPURE COUNTRY GRAVY

Makes 2 cups (480 ml)

SCIENTISTS BELIEVE THAT THE COLLISION OF WATER, flour, and heat originally formed the essential building block of the universe. We can re-create that miraculous moment in our own kitchen laboratories each time we make this savory Superpure Country Gravy.

1 Begin the gravy by adding the oil and flour to a medium saucepan over medium heat. Whisk constantly for 3 minutes, or until the flour is lightly toasted. Add the spices while continuing to whisk for another minute. Pour the soy milk and liquid smoke into the pan and increase the heat, bring the sauce to a boil, and cook until it thickens, whisking constantly. Reduce the heat to low and cover until ready to serve.

¼ cup (60 ml) canola oil

¼ cup (30 g) all-purpose flour

½ teaspoon dried sage

½ teaspoon garlic powder

½ teaspoon onion powder

½ teaspoon salt

½ teaspoon black pepper

1½ cups (360 ml) unsweetened soy milk

½ teaspoon liquid smoke

NATURALISTIC CORN GRAVY

Makes 2 cups (480 ml)

WITH CORN BEING ONE OF THE MOST NATURAL foods still in existence, we are always looking for new ways to incorporate the golden kernels into our taco journey. One of the best ways we've found to increase consumption of many vegetables is to blend them into a gravy. Corn is no exception. Apply this gravy to your taco when a sweet, creamy note will benefit the taco profile. For instance, Naturalistic Corn Gravy pairs well with Sincere Sriracha-Agave Tenders (page 102).

2 tablespoons canola oil
½ yellow onion, diced
1 green bell pepper, diced
½ cup (120 ml) vegetable broth
½ cup (120 ml) unsweetened soy milk
2 tablespoons cornstarch
2 cups (240 g) frozen corn kernels
½ teaspoon black pepper
½ teaspoon dried sage
½ teaspoon salt

1 In a medium saucepan, sauté the onion and pepper in the oil over medium-high heat for 5 minutes.

2 In a small bowl, combine the broth and soy milk and slowly sprinkle cornstarch into it while whisking constantly to create a slurry.

3 Add the slurry, corn, spices, and salt to the saucepan. Increase the heat, bring the sauce to a boil, and cook until it thickens, whisking constantly. Use an immersion blender to puree the gravy to your desired consistency.

REGENERATIVE RED ONIONS

Makes about ½ cup (120 ml)

1 red onion
¼ cup (60 ml) white wine vinegar (or apple cider vinegar)
¼ cup (60 ml) lime juice
1½ teaspoons salt

FOR EONS PEOPLE HAVE BELIEVED that fermented vegetables enhance bodily functions. We have even read that pickles can stave off diseases like moosebumps. Who knows what these pickled onions can do for you? They are a great topping on just about any taco and will keep for weeks in your fridge. Just make sure to store them in a glass or ceramic container.

1 Bring a small pot of water to a boil. Meanwhile, slice the onion into thin rounds. Make the pickling mixture by adding the vinegar, lime juice, and salt to a glass or ceramic bowl or jar, cover tightly, and shake it to mix.

2 When the water boils, drop the onion slices in the water for about 15 seconds. Fish them out with a slotted spoon and add them to the pickling mixture. Cover and put the container in the fridge. Shake it up every so often making sure the onions are fully covered. You can use them after a half hour, but they will be better the next day. They will last at least 2 weeks, if you don't eat them all.

HIGH-VIBRATION KALE CHIPS

Fills 8 tacos

IT WAS PREVIOUSLY THOUGHT THAT KALE CHIPS needed to be dehydrated below 118°F (87°C) in specialized equipment to preserve the delicate phytoenergies. We have recently discovered that such excessive uncooking time actually attenuates the frequency of the kale at the cellular level. This updated technique reduces preparation time significantly and maintains the highest vibration possible. We use a salad spinner to remove all moisture and a common domestic oven to increase drying time. This produces a superiorly crisp kale chip with a resonance that your soul can feel. Sprinkle these High-Vibration Kale Chips on softer-textured taco fillings such as Sincere Sriracha-Agave Tenders (page 102).

1 bunch kale
1 tablespoon olive oil
¼ cup (15 g) nutritional yeast
1 teaspoon garlic powder
¼ teaspoon salt

1 Preheat the oven to 300°F (150°C).

2 Wash and thoroughly dry the kale leaves, using a salad spinner if you have one. Remove the stems and toss the leaves into a large bowl. Drizzle the oil over the kale and sprinkle the nutritional yeast, garlic powder, and salt on top. Massage the kale until evenly coated, tearing the leaves in the process. Let the kale know it is appreciated. Arrange the leaves in a single layer on a dry baking sheet. Bake for 25 minutes, stirring once halfway through. Allow the chips to cool for 5 minutes to maximize crispness.

ENZYMATIC ESCABECHE

Makes about 4 cups (960 ml)

THE VINEGAR IN THIS PICKLE WILL INCREASE the activity of naturally occurring enzymes. It's common knowledge that these enzymes manifest themselves through your health. So do not hesitate to add these pickles as a garnish to your favorite tacos.

1 Bring the vinegar, water, salt, and sugar to boil in a medium saucepan. While the vinegar mixture heats, slice the onion halves most of the way through from top to root end, being careful to keep the root end intact. Then slice the onion into half rings. You should end up with thin slices of onion, each about an inch long or less.

2 Once the vinegar mixture boils, add the onion matchsticks, garlic, bay leaf, and peppercorns. Reduce the heat to low and simmer 2 minutes. Turn off the heat and add the remaining ingredients. Transfer everything to a glass dish or jar, cover, and refrigerate for at least 4 hours. This keeps refrigerated for 2 weeks.

2 cups (480 ml) white vinegar
1 cup (240 ml) water
2 tablespoons salt
1 tablespoon light brown sugar
½ white onion, sliced from root to top
2 garlic cloves
1 bay leaf
½ tablespoon whole peppercorns
10 ounces (280 g) carrots in matchsticks
1 jalapeño, cut in matchsticks

SUPER CLEANSE: Look for bagged carrot matchsticks in the produce area of your grocery store. If you can't find them, for heaven's sake don't spend all day shredding carrots. Cut them into any bite-size shape you prefer, and use jalapeño rings and onion half moons.

ARTIST TACOS

There's a cafe in Austin, Cherrywood Coffeehouse, that sells "Artist Tacos," tacos that you make yourself by choosing from a list of ingredients. We've always thought this was an apt description. In the Taco Cleanse we talk a lot about the science behind tacos, but there's also a lot of artistry that goes into crafting the perfect taco.

This chapter offers a few suggestions for complete tacos. If you're new to eating tacos, either recreationally or faithfully, use it as training wheels before assembling your own taco creations. Once you've gotten the hang of combining a tortilla, a few fillings, and a condiment or two, head back to the previous chapters and be your own artist. Remember that you must crawl before you walk, and you must walk before you go around making tacos on your own.

Start here. You can easily make thirty days of meals out of the Artist Tacos. In fact, you can thrive on a diet of these recipes alone. There is something for every meal: breakfast, lunch, dinner, fourth meal, and dessert (don't forget to visit the Supplements chapter often). Some of these recipes may introduce a paradigm shift to your body-mind. Do not be afraid to try something new! The Taco Cleanse isn't about fearing the unknown; it's about becoming an artist.

FULL-SPECTRUM TACOS

~~~

Makes 8 tacos

AN IMPORTANT PART OF THE TACO CLEANSE is the act of celebration. We created this recipe to celebrate the passing of gay marriage, state by state. Now that that's no longer necessary, make it for Pride. Or any day. Love wins. Concentrate on each of the colors as you ingest their nutrimatter and connect with their vibrant, healing energies.

1 Fill each tortilla with the fillings in parallel lines that follow the color order of a rainbow.

½ cup Essential Pico de Gallo (page 115)

½ cup Enzymatic Escabeche (page 136)

1 cup Rewarding Esquites (page 68)

1 cup Radiant Rajas (page 65)

1 batch Blue Corn Chip–Crusted Tofu (page 90)

2 cups Abundant Roasted Potatoes (page 74), made with purple potatoes

8 tortillas (corn or flour, you choose. No judgment.)

TROPICAL BREAKFAST TACO

Makes 1 taco

THIS IS THE TACO FOR EATING IN A HAMMOCK while dreaming of the Caribbean. Gallo Pinto, a hearty filling, marries with sweet fried plantains for a combination that will rock your socks off. Top that with Guacamole Viridis and rest it on a corn tortilla blanket, and you will be assured a tropical contact high. Well-known Taco Cleanse participant John Stamos enjoys his tropical breakfast tacos with a side of Salsa Inglesa.

1   This recipe comes together super easily if you make the rice and beans for the Gallo Pinto and the Salsa Inglesa the day before. Then, just make the guacamole, sauté the Gallo Pinto, and fry the plantains for a fabulous taco.

⅓ cup Gallo Pinto (page 88)

1 tablespoon Guacamole Viridis (page 126)

1 teaspoon Spirited Salsa Inglesa (page 116), optional

2 pieces Fried Plantains (page 67)

1 Corn Tortilla (page 49) or store-bought

GREEN CHILE POZOLE

Makes 8 to 10 tacos

IDEALLY YOU WOULD MAKE THESE TACOS WITH roasted Hatch peppers, known to resonate to the vibration of life. But those special snowflakes are only around for a month in the late summer and we need to eat tacos any time of year, so Anaheim chiles will work.

1 Preheat the broiler. Broil the chiles until the skins are at least 75 percent charred, rotating them with tongs every couple of minutes, and then set aside in a folded paper bag or a tightly sealed bowl to steam for at least 10 minutes.

2 Spread the tomatillos, jalapeño, onions, and garlic on a baking sheet and broil for about 5 minutes. Wearing gloves, rub the skins off the Anaheim chiles and remove the stem and seeds from them and the jalapeño. Put the Anaheim chiles, tomatillos, jalapeño, onions, and garlic in the food processor and process until the mixture is the consistency of salsa. Pour

3 Anaheim chiles

12 ounces (340 g) tomatillos

1 jalapeño

2 small white onions, quartered

3 garlic cloves, peeled

1 teaspoon salt

1 cup (25 g) Soy Curls, crumbled

15 ounces (425 g) hominy

½ teaspoon oregano

½ teaspoon cumin

1 cup (225 g) baby spinach

½ cup (25 g) cilantro

1 tablespoon lime juice

Salt and black pepper

¼ cup (35 g) toasted pumpkin seeds

2 scallions, chopped

8 to 10 Flour or Corn Tortillas (page 47 or 49) or store-bought

into a large saucepan along with the salt, Soy Curls, hominy, oregano, and cumin. Cook over low heat for 20 minutes, stirring occasionally. Stir in the spinach until it wilts. Turn off the heat and stir in the cilantro and lime juice. Add salt and pepper to taste. Top with the toasted pumpkin seeds and scallions and serve on the tortillas.

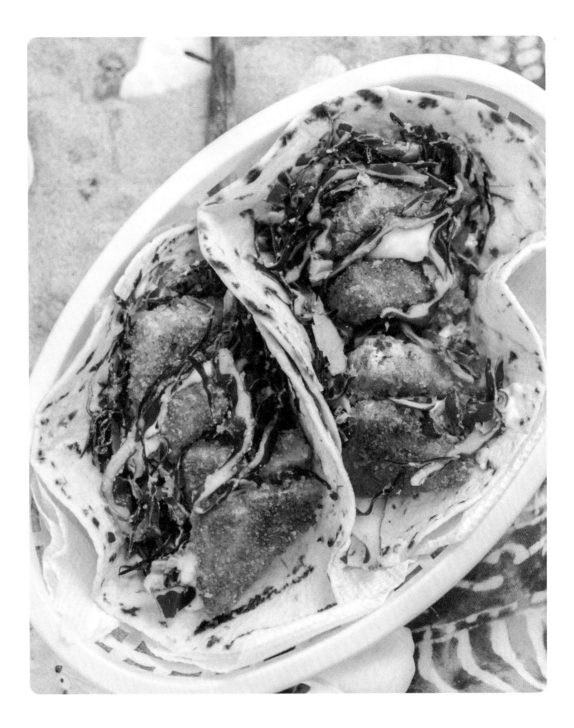

INFINITE FISH TACOS

Makes 8 tacos

1 batch Bright Light Baja Slaw (page 55)

8 Flour Tortillas (page 47) or store-bought

1 batch Iridescent Fried Tofu (page 92)

1 batch Tartar Sauce (page 124)

CLOSE YOUR EYES AND LISTEN to the hypnotic sound of the ocean as you eat this taco. Holding a seashell up to your ear will help.

SUPER CLEANSE: Replace the fried tofu with Sophie's Kitchen Breaded Vegan Fish Fillets.

1 Place about ½ cup of slaw in each tortilla. Top with two pieces of fried tofu and a dollop of tartar sauce.

HACK YOUR TACO CLEANSE: In the summer, leave your slow cooker outside in the sun to avoid heating up the kitchen!

TATER TOT-CHO TACOS

Makes 6 tacos

SURELY YOU HAVE TASTED THE PERFECTION that is nachos, but have you tried swapping the tortilla chips for tater tots yet? That brilliant food experience can be made even more perfect by putting your tot-chos in a taco. The ultimate comfort food, made portable.

1 Bake the tater tots according to package directions. While they bake, gather the other fillings. In each flour tortilla, place 6 tater tots as the bottom layer. Top with chorizo, nacho cheese, crema, guacamole, and tomato. Garnish with cilantro and scallions. Add pickled jalapeños, if using, to taste.

One 16-ounce (454 g) bag frozen tater tots

6 Flour Tortillas (page 47) or store-bought

1 cup (240 ml) Tolerant Bulgur Chorizo (page 78) or store-bought soyrizo

Elevated Nacho Cheese (page 130) or store-bought, such as Teese Nacho Cheese

6 tablespoons Cashew Crema (page 125) or store-bought, such as Tofutti Sour Supreme

6 tablespoons Guacamole Viridis (page 126) or store-bought guacamole

1 medium tomato, diced

2 tablespoons cilantro, chopped

2 tablespoons chopped scallions

2 tablespoons chopped pickled jalapeños, optional

SMOKED BRISKET AND JALAPEÑO MAC AND CHEESE TACOS

Makes 16 tacos

A TACO STUDENT ASKED, "Which vegan cheese sauce is the best with macaroni?" The taco scientist replied, "You cannot find a vegan cheese sauce that is not the best." With this understanding, the student was cleansed. Since the discovery of nutritional yeast in 1975, the early cheese sauce has ceaselessly evolved and deviated in myriad directions. Here, you are invited to use either jalapeño-infused cheese sauce variation. Current food-combining theory suggests that this transformative macaroni and cheese and BBQ seitan brisket be paired together on a flour tortilla.

1 Preheat the oven to 350°F (175°C). Oil an 8 x 8-inch (20 x 20 cm) cake pan.

2 To make the seitan, combine 1 cup BBQ sauce, broth, oil, and soy sauce in a large bowl and whisk thoroughly. Sprinkle the vital wheat gluten into the liquid mixture and knead by hand until just combined. The dough will be soft but not shaggy. Flatten the dough into the prepared pan and cover with aluminum foil. Bake for 60 minutes, flipping the seitan at the 30-minute mark and covering again with foil.

(Recipe continues . . .)

BBQ brisket

2 cups (470 ml) Breakthrough BBQ Sauce (page 126) or store-bought BBQ sauce

1 cup (240 ml) vegetable broth

2 tablespoons canola oil

2 tablespoons soy sauce

2 cups (260 g) vital wheat gluten

Macaroni and cheese

16 ounces (454 g) elbow pasta

1 batch Minimalist Nacho Cheese (page 128) or Elevated Nacho Cheese (page 130)

2 tablespoons diced pickled jalapeños

16 Flour Tortillas (page 47) or store-bought

3 While the seitan cooks, boil pasta in a large pot according to package directions. Drain, rinse with cold water, and return pasta to the pot. Fold the cheesy sauce and jalapeños into the pot of drained pasta and set aside.

4 Move the cooked seitan to a cutting board and slice thinly. Return the seitan slices to the casserole dish and toss them with remaining BBQ sauce.

5 Fill the tortillas with mac and cheese and BBQ brisket. Garnish with more BBQ sauce or sriracha.

 TIP This BBQ seitan provides maximum benefits when smoked on a charcoal grill. Soak a handful of wood chips in warm water for at least 30 minutes, drain, and toss directly onto 250°F (120°C) coals. Place the prebaked slab of seitan on the grill for an hour with the lid closed and the bottom vents opened. Repeat the mantra "Low and slow" during the smoking process.

> SUPER CLEANSE: You can use bottled BBQ sauce to save a little time. Thicker sauces may need to be thinned out with water or vegetable broth.

HACK YOUR TACO CLEANSE: Warm your tortillas on the dashboard of your car on the way to a summer barbecue! Alternatively, have heated seats in your car? You now have a portable tortilla warmer!

MEXICAN CHOPPED SALAD TACOS

Makes 8 tacos

THE SPECIAL AMINO ACID PROFILE of this taco

results in the perfect antioxidant-oxidant ratio.

1 Whisk together the vinaigrette ingredients until emulsified.

2 Combine the salad ingredients in a large bowl. Drizzle on the vinaigrette and thoroughly mix together. (The salad and vinaigrette can be made in advance, but do not mix the two until the last minute.) Divide among the 8 tortillas. Serve immediately.

Cumin-lime vinaigrette

¼ cup (60 ml) olive oil

2 tablespoons lime juice

½ tablespoon agave nectar

¼ teaspoon cumin

1 garlic clove, minced

Large pinch of salt

Salad

2 cups (85 g) chopped romaine lettuce

12 cherry tomatoes, halved

Kernels sliced from 1 ear of corn, or ¾ cup (130 g) thawed frozen corn

½ medium avocado, chopped

½ cup (85 g) cooked black beans

¼ cup (45 g) chopped bell pepper

¼ cup (40 g) chopped jicama

2 tablespoons diced red onion

2 tablespoons chopped cilantro

8 Corn Tortillas (page 49) or store-bought

FRITO PIE TACOS

Makes 8 tacos

CAN A PIE BE A TACO? Is Frito pie even a pie? Does Frito pie translate to "fried foot"? These are the things you must contemplate while you eat the Frito Pie Taco.

1 Heat the oil over medium heat in a medium saucepan. Add the onion and cook until soft, about 5 minutes. Add the garlic and sauté for 30 seconds, or until fragrant. Add the bulgur and spices and stir thoroughly. Add the soy sauce, tomato paste, and diced tomatoes. Fill one of the tomato cans with water and add it to the pot, twice. Cover and bring to a simmer. Reduce the heat to low and cook for 20 minutes, stirring occasionally. After 20 minutes, check the chili. If it's still fairly wet, uncover and cook until most of the moisture is absorbed, another 5 minutes or so.

2 Warm the tortillas. Add the chili and a handful of corn chips to each taco. Serve the garnishes, if using, on the side so guests can top their tacos as they prefer.

Chili

1 tablespoon cooking oil

1 large onion, chopped

4 garlic cloves, chopped

1 cup (240 g) bulgur, texturized vegetable protein, or a combination of the two

1 tablespoon chili powder

2 teaspoons oregano

2 teaspoons ground cumin

1 teaspoon paprika

1 teaspoon cayenne, optional

6 tablespoons soy sauce or tamari

6 tablespoons tomato paste

Two 10-ounce (283 g) cans diced tomatoes with green chiles, such as Ro-Tel brand (mild or your preference)

Water, to fill an empty 10-ounce can twice

Everything else

8 Flour Tortillas (page 47) or store-bought

Corn chips, such as Fritos

Chopped white onion, optional

Chopped tomato, optional

Shredded vegan cheddar, optional

Cashew Crema (page 125) or store-bought vegan sour cream, optional

ELEVATED SONORAN HOT DOG TACOS

Makes 8 tacos

QUASH ANY SECRET LONGINGS YOU MAY HAVE for fluffy, bready, yeasty hot dog buns with this traditional New Mexican taco. These 'dogs are frequently served at small food stands or carts with a grilled jalapeño on the side. Studies have shown an exponential increase in levels after eating this taco, especially when supplemented with a Beergarita.

1 Cook the hot dogs according to package directions or using your preferred method. Slice in half lengthwise. Spread a line of vegan mayo down the middle of each tortilla. Add half a hot dog, a slice of avocado, and the bacon, if using. Top with the chorizo, beans, cheese, mustard, and pico de gallo.

4 vegan hot dogs

8 Corn or Flour Tortillas (page 47 or 49) or store-bought, warmed

Mayo from Rewarding Esquites (page 68) or store-bought vegan mayo

1 avocado, sliced

1 cup Foundational Tempeh Bacon (page 105), chopped into small pieces, optional

1 cup Tolerant Bulgur Chorizo (page 78) or store-bought vegan chorizo, cooked

1 cup (170 g) warm cooked black beans or pinto beans, optional

Vegan cheese, optional

Yellow mustard

½ cup Essential Pico de Gallo (page 115)

HEALING JALAPEÑO POPPER TACOS

Makes 6 to 8 tacos

EVEN THE MOST DEDICATED TACO CLEANSER might occasionally get a cold. This is the perfect taco to cleanse your sinuses and your aura. Beginner taco cleansers might want to tamp down the heat a bit by removing the membranes (the white stuff) and seeds from the jalapeños. Don't be a hero.

1 Microwave the red bell pepper with a splash of water for 2 minutes, or until soft, and drain. Add to a blender with all the other bean spread ingredients except the water and blend until smooth. Add water 1 tablespoon at a time until the bean mixture is spreadable but not runny.

2 Heat the oil in a large sauté pan over medium-high heat. Open a window or turn on a fan to ventilate your cooking space. Sauté the bell pepper and jalapeños for 5 minutes, or until tender.

3 Heat the tortillas using your preferred method. Spread a layer of cheesy bean spread on each. Add a few cooked jalapeños and garnish with cornflakes.

Cheesy bean spread

¼ red bell pepper, sliced

One 15-ounce (425 g) can butter beans, drained and rinsed (about 1½ cups)

2 tablespoons nutritional yeast

2 tablespoons tahini

1 tablespoon white miso

1 tablespoon lemon juice

1½ teaspoons chili powder

1½ teaspoons oregano

1 teaspoon cumin

1 teaspoon ground mustard

2 to 4 tablespoons water

Everything else

1 tablespoon canola oil

½ pound (227 g) green bell pepper, capped, seeded, and sliced into strips

¼ pound (114 g) jalapeños, capped and sliced into strips

6 to 8 Flour or Corn Tortillas (page 47 or 49) or store-bought

Cornflakes

SUPREME BACON, SCRAMBLE, AND CHEESE TACOS

Makes 8 tacos

BREAKFAST TACOS ARE A KEY COMPONENT of the Taco Cleanse. If you start the day off right, good habits are sure to follow. You can make the ingredients for this taco the night before so the first taco of the day is ready in no time. This is such a simple taco, you might be tempted to add more ingredients. Resist the temptation. Eating a taco is its own reward.

1 Warm the tortillas. Spoon the tofu scramble and bacon onto each tortilla. Add a sprinkle of cheese or a spoonful of cheesy sauce. Do not add more ingredients. Eat. Taco.

8 Corn or Flour Tortillas (page 49 or 47) or store-bought

1 cup (240 ml) Foundational Tempeh Bacon (page 105) or 16 slices store-bought vegan bacon

2 cups (480 ml) Wake and Shake Scramble (page 96)

½ cup (120 ml) shredded vegan cheddar, Minimalist Nacho Cheese (page 128), or Elevated Nacho Cheese (page 130)

ACCELERATED BREAKFAST TACO

Makes 1 taco

1 Flour Tortilla (page 47) or store-bought
1 spoonful peanut butter
¼ cup breakfast cereal, optional
1 ripe banana

EARLY IN THE MORNING, we often prioritize sleep over a balanced breakfast taco. If you have hit the snooze button once too many times, consider the Accelerated Breakfast Taco. You can assemble this taco quickly using common kitchen staples. We encourage you to improvise and start your day on the right path.

1 Microwave the tortilla for 15 seconds. Gently apply the peanut butter evenly onto the tortilla. Sprinkle the cereal evenly over the tortilla. Peel the banana. Center the peeled banana on the tortilla. Fold tortilla in half lengthwise along banana and apply even pressure. Go!

ENERGIZING DUTCH WAFFLE TACOS

Makes 4 Dutch tacos

4 Waffle Tortillas (page 53)

8 cooked vegan sausage patties, such as Lightlife Gimme Lean Sausage

2 tablespoons maple syrup

2 tablespoons vegan margarine, such as Earth Balance

WHEN TACO SCIENTISTS TRAVEL TO PORTLAND, our first stop is often to the Flavour Spot for Dutch Tacos. This exotic breakfast consists of a waffle folded in half, cradling vegan sausages and slathered with maple butter. Upon our safe return, we knew we would re-create this delicacy in the comfort of our Austin homes. Use a "classic" (non-Belgian) waffle iron to achieve the proper taco fold.

1 Prepare 4 sheets of aluminum foil slightly larger than the waffle. Place a waffle on each sheet. Place 2 sausage patties on half of each waffle. Drizzle syrup and melted margarine to taste. Fold the waffles in half along with the foil. Seal the top and one side of the foil to retain warmth while consuming.

THANKFUL SWEET POTATO PIE TACOS

Makes 4 tacos

PRACTICING GRATITUDE is an important aspect of a detoxified lifestyle. We have found that the best way to get into a thankful mindset is by eating Thanksgiving-inspired tacos. Here we offer the Sweet Potato Pie Taco. Like pumpkin, sweet potato sparkles when accompanied by warm spices like cinnamon, nutmeg, clove, and allspice. While the sweet potato spice latte may never come to fruition, we can be thankful that the Sweet Potato Pie Taco is available year-round.

For the candied pecans:

1 Preheat the oven to 300°F (150°C). Line a baking sheet with parchment paper or a silicone baking mat.

2 Whisk together the water and cornstarch in a medium-large bowl. Add the sugar, cinnamon, molasses, salt, and vanilla extract. Work the mixture together with a rubber spatula until

(Recipe continues . . .)

Candied pecans

1 tablespoon water

½ teaspoon cornstarch

½ cup (106 g) sugar

½ teaspoon cinnamon

¼ teaspoon molasses

¼ teaspoon salt

¼ teaspoon vanilla extract

1 cup (125 g) pecan pieces

Sweet potato filling

1 tablespoon canola oil, plus more for the baking sheet

1 tablespoon maple syrup

½ teaspoon cinnamon

¼ teaspoon nutmeg

¼ teaspoon salt

1 large sweet potato, peeled and diced into ¼-inch (0.5 cm) cubes

4 Flour Tortillas (page 47) or store-bought

completely combined. The consistency should resemble wet sand. Fold in the pecan pieces until evenly coated. Spread the pecan slurry thinly on the lined baking sheet. Bake for 40 minutes, stirring once halfway through. Slide the pecans while still on the parchment paper over to a cooling rack and allow to cool completely. Crumble the cooled candied pecans into bite-sized pieces.

For the sweet potato filling:

1 Preheat the oven to 400°F (200°C). Oil a baking sheet.

2 Whisk together the oil, syrup, cinnamon, nutmeg, and salt in a large bowl. Add the diced sweet potatoes and toss until evenly coated. Arrange in a single layer on the oiled baking sheet. Bake for 40 minutes, stirring once halfway through.

3 Assemble sweet potatoes and candied pecans on each tortilla. Enjoy!

TIP Spread a spoonful of vegan cream cheese onto the warmed flour tortilla prior to assembling your dessert taco to enhance its flavorful nature.

HACK YOUR TACO CLEANSE: Keep tortillas warm in an electric blanket while making breakfast tacos in bed!

INSPIRING CHURRO-WAFFLE TACOS

Makes 3 churro-waffle tacos

WE AT TACO HEADQUARTERS have a fondness for churros, but there are inherent issues preventing churro consumption on a Taco Cleanse. Deep-fryer temperatures can be finicky and splattering oil can be painful. Most relevant to our concerns, a churro is not a taco. The crunchy fritters emerge from the hot oil as a star-shaped extrusion, void of taco benefits. We have reformulated the batter to work in a waffle iron, allowing the finished churro to be folded in half. Fill your cinnamon-kissed churro taco with a banana and agave nectar to maintain peak levels.

1 On a shallow plate, whisk together ¼ cup (53 g) sugar and ¼ teaspoon cinnamon and set aside. Whisk together the cornstarch, flour, baking powder, salt, remaining ¼ cup sugar, and ¼ teaspoon cinnamon in a large bowl. Add the water and oil to the bowl and stir until just combined. Follow your waffle iron's directions to cook the waffles, using ⅔ cup (160 ml) of the batter for each. Press one side of each cooked waffle into the plate of cinnamon sugar while still warm. With the sugar side up, lay 2 banana halves side by side on one half of the waffle. Drizzle with agave nectar and fold waffle in half to cradle the bananas.

Tortillas

½ cup (106 g) sugar

½ teaspoon cinnamon

2 teaspoons cornstarch

1 cup (120 g) all-purpose flour

1 teaspoon baking powder

¼ teaspoon salt

1 cup (240 ml) water

¼ cup (60 ml) canola oil

¼ cup (60 ml) agave nectar

Fillings

3 bananas, sliced in half lengthwise

Agave nectar

CHOCOLATE-RASPBERRY DESSERT TACOS

Makes 10 tacos

OUR FRIEND and amazing baker Kristen Davenport runs Capital City Bakery in Austin, Texas. She is an old pro at taco cleansing. When Kristen realized that some people might assume that dessert wasn't allowed on the Taco Cleanse, she jumped straight into the kitchen to make these tacos. So now you have no excuse to slip off the Taco Cleanse when you're tempted by the siren song of chocolate.

For the raspberry preserves:

1 Combine all the preserve ingredients in a medium-size saucepan over medium heat. Stir intermittently until the preserves thicken to the consistency of jam. Allow to cool.

For the chocolate ganache:

1 In a microwave-safe bowl, heat the chocolate chips and oil on high for

Raspberry preserves
1 cup (125 g) frozen or fresh raspberries
6 tablespoons (80 g) sugar
1 tablespoon cornstarch

Easy chocolate ganache
½ cup (88 g) semisweet chocolate chips
2 tablespoons (30 ml) cooking oil

Soft taco shell
1 tablespoon (13 g) sugar
¼ teaspoon vanilla extract
⅓ cup (75 ml) almond milk
1 tablespoon (15 ml) cooking oil
¼ cup (30 g) all-purpose flour
¼ teaspoon baking powder
⅛ teaspoon salt
½ teaspoon cornstarch

Powdered sugar

90 seconds, or until melted. Stir well to combine.

(Recipe continues . . .)

For the taco shells:

1 Preheat your griddle on high, approximately 350 to 400°F (175 to 200°C). If using a stovetop griddle, heat to medium. A tabletop griddle will work better than a stovetop griddle.

2 Whisk the sugar, vanilla extract, almond milk, and oil together in a medium bowl. Combine the flour, baking powder, salt, and cornstarch in a separate bowl. Whisk the dry ingredients into the wet ingredients, one half at a time. The batter shouldn't be too thick. Add more almond milk if necessary.

3 Once the griddle has heated up, pour on a tablespoon of batter. Using the back of your tablespoon, smooth out the batter to a circle about 3 inches wide. You should be able to see the griddle through the batter. Let the batter cook on one side for 1 to 3 minutes, until lightly browned. Small bubbles should appear on the uncooked surface and the shell should be fairly thin. Flip using a spatula and allow the other side to cook completely. Transfer to a plate.

4 Fold each taco shell in half, stuff with the raspberry preserves, drizzle with the chocolate ganache, and sprinkle with powdered sugar. You should be able to pick up your taco, but we won't judge you if you eat it with a fork (poser).

5 Store any leftover jam covered tightly in the refrigerator for about a week.

VARIATIONS:

Seasonal Berry: Replace the raspberries with any other berry.

Bananas Foster: Stuff with caramelized banana slices and top with caramel sauce and brown sugar.

Mexican Hot Chocolate: Add 2 tablespoons cocoa powder and 1 teaspoon cayenne to your soft taco shell batter. Stuff the cooked shells with melted vegan marshmallows or vegan marshmallow fluff, drizzle with chocolate ganache, and sprinkle with cinnamon and cayenne.

Birthday Tacos: Stuff the shells with strawberry preserves, drizzle with sugar glaze (mix 1 cup powdered sugar, ½ teaspoon almond extract, and 1 tablespoon water until it forms a thin sauce), and top with rainbow sprinkles and a candle.

Biscoff Tacos: Stuff the taco shell with Biscoff cookie spread, top with sugar glaze (see Birthday Tacos above), cinnamon, and Biscoff cookie crumbs.

HORCHATA ICE CREAM TACOS

Makes 6 tacos

IF YOU AREN'T LUCKY ENOUGH to live near an ice cream parlor that serves vegan ice cream tacos, there's still hope because now you can make your own. Accidentally vegan waffle bowls can be found near the ice cream cones at many grocery stores or ordered from online grocers such as Amazon.

If you don't have leftover rice, combine 1 cup rice, 1½ cups water, and ½ teaspoon salt in a small saucepan. Bring to a boil, then cover and turn the heat to low. Simmer covered for 15 minutes. Then move the pan off the heat and let sit, covered, for another 10 minutes.

1 The night before, place your ice cream maker insert in the freezer.

2 Combine the rice milk, brown sugar, agave nectar, oil, and cinnamon in a medium saucepan. Bring to a boil and then turn down to a simmer for 1 minute. As it simmers, beat with a wire whisk

½ cup (360 ml) rice milk
½ cup (72 g) brown sugar
¼ cup (60 ml) agave nectar
¼ cup (60 ml) canola oil
1 teaspoon cinnamon
1 cup (200 g) cooked long grain rice
6 waffle bowls
¼ cup (60 ml) sliced almonds
¼ cup (60 ml) puffed rice cereal

so that the oil and sugar are thoroughly incorporated into the mixture. Let the mixture cool, then refrigerate for at least 2 hours.

3 Mix the rice milk mixture and cooked rice in your ice cream maker, following the manufacturer's instructions. After about 20 minutes, with the ice cream maker turned off, you should be able to run a spoon through the ice cream and leave a furrow.

4 While the ice cream mixes, wrap a damp paper towel around each waffle bowl and microwave for 20 seconds. Being careful not to burn yourself with the steam

(Recipe continues . . .)

from the paper towel, quickly mold the waffle bowl into a taco shell shape. You might find it helpful to drape each waffle shell over the handle of a wooden spoon. Set aside waffle shells until ice cream is ready.

5 Spoon ice cream into each waffle taco shell. Spoon sliced almonds and puffed rice onto the taco, pressing with clean fingers or the back of the spoon so they stick firmly into the ice cream. Place tacos in the freezer on a plate or cookie sheet lined with wax paper to firm.

> SUPER CLEANSE: No time to make your own ice cream? Use your favorite nondairy vanilla ice cream and top with dark chocolate chips.

SUPPLEMENTS

Supplements are key to the Taco Cleanse, especially at the Fuego level. When you drink alcohol, your liver enters detoxification mode. The alcohol creates a toxic aura in your spleen that collects other toxins for elimination. This isn't anything new. How often have you heard someone tell you to take "the hair of the dog that bit you?"

Besides its detoxifying properties, alcohol also raises your cortisol levels. Cortisol is an important intransitive fluid that activates antistress pathways and fights inflammation.

But not all alcohols are equal. Tequila, made from blue agave, contains the highest concentration of phytoelements. Just like bourbon only comes from Kentucky and champagne only comes from the Champagne region of France, true tequila is only made in the area surrounding Tequila in Jalisco. Like all foods made only in one place, it's a superfood. Science hasn't yet been able to explain this phenomenon, but we're working to prove that it's true.

FUNDAMENTAL MARGARITA

Makes 1 drink

WINTER IS APPROACHING and you want to boost your levels before the holiday season. A huge mistake people make when they're facing the social pressures of the holiday season or an upcoming costume party is loading up on Supplements, thinking they can bypass the harder work of a real Taco Cleanse. But that's setting yourself up for failure. Supplements only work when combined with a rigorous course of tacos.

Kosher salt

1 ounce (30 ml) lime juice, plus a lime wedge for serving

Ice cubes

2 ounces (60 ml) silver tequila

1 ounce (30 ml) orange liqueur, such as Cointreau

1 Put some kosher salt on a saucer. Run a cut wedge of lime around the top of your margarita glass, remove it, and then dip the top of the glass into the saucer. Lift up, tap to remove excessive salt, and then stand it upright, garnishing with the lime wedge. Add ice to the cup. Then add the tequila, lime juice, and orange liqueur.

AGAVE MARGARITA

Makes 1 drink

THIS MARGARITA IS PACKED WITH ANTIOXIDANTS to promote an oxygen-rich liver. Exercise your right to glow! The agave is great for giving you the energy that you'll need to get through your night . . . or day. There is no judgment on the Taco Cleanse.

1 Quarter two of the limes and add them to a mason jar or cocktail shaker along with the orange quarters. Muddle the fruit along with the tequila and agave nectar and pour over ice into a cocktail glass. If you like, you can strain out the orange and lime peels, but it isn't necessary. Garnish with extra lime.

3 limes
1 small orange, quartered
¼ cup (60 ml) silver tequila
1 tablespoon agave nectar
Ice cubes

AVOCADO MARGARITA

Makes 2 drinks

IF YOU'VE BEEN FOLLOWING a low-fat, low-alcohol, low-carb diet, this margarita, inspired by the Austin restaurant Curra's, will help get your body on track with the Taco Cleanse. It's also great for people transitioning from green smoothies.

1 Crush the ice in the blender first and then blend until finely ground. Then add the tequila, avocado, orange liqueur, orange juice, and lime juice in a blender. Blend until as smooth as possible; add more lime juice if necessary to keep the blender moving.

2 In the meantime, pour some salt into a saucer. Run a cut wedge of lime around the top of the glass, remove it, and then dip the top of the glass into the saucer. Lift up, tap to remove excess salt, and then stand it upright, garnishing with a lime wedge. Pour in the margarita mix and enjoy.

3 cups (140 g) ice cubes

¾ cup (180 ml) tequila

1 avocado, cubed

¼ cup (60 ml) orange liqueur, such as Cointreau

½ cup (120 ml) orange juice (preferably freshly squeezed)

Juice of three limes, plus one more for serving

Salt for the glass

REHYDRATING WATERITA

Makes 1 drink

4 ounces (120 ml) watermelon juice (see instructions below)

2 ounces (60 ml) silver tequila

1 ounce (30 ml) melon liqueur, such as Midori

Ice cubes

SHHH. LISTEN. REALLY LISTEN. You hear that? It's your body. It needs watermelon. A watermelon margarita, to be exact. Novice taco cleanser Lance, a student from Denton, Texas, shares a story we've heard so often: "I was just eating whatever was in front of me without really thinking about it. A salad one day. Soup another. Until one day, I found myself faced with a fruit salad. But I just couldn't bring myself to eat it. My body was crying out for something better. I threw aside the fruit salad and grabbed a Waterita. That was the first day of the rest of my life."

1 To make watermelon juice, puree watermelon (seedless or with the seeds removed) and pass through a sieve. Discard the pulp or save for another use.

2 Combine with tequila and melon liqueur and pour over ice.

SPARKLING WATERITA

Makes 1 drink

3 ounces (90 ml) watermelon juice

3 ounces (90 ml) citrus soda (Sprite, 7 Up, Fresca, Squirt)

Ice cubes

1 Combine the watermelon juice and soda and pour over ice.

EVERYDAY MEXICAN MARTINI

Makes 1 drink

OUR CULTURE HAS AN UNHEALTHY ATTITUDE toward drinking. "I had a hard day today," you might say to yourself. "I deserve a drink." Get this flawed thinking out of your mind! It's crucial to supplement on the Taco Cleanse, so don't limit yourself to drinking only when you've had a hard day or when there's a birthday to celebrate. Your body deserves the best.

1 Combine everything but the olives in a drink shaker with plenty of ice. Shake,

2 ounces (60 ml) silver tequila

2 ounces (60 ml) orange liqueur, such as Cointreau

2 ounces (60 ml) lime juice

Splash of orange juice

Splash of olive brine (from a jar of olives)

Generous pour of citrus soda (Sprite, 7 Up, Fresca, Squirt)

Ice cubes

Green olives

shake, shake. Strain into a glass and garnish with at least two olives. Seriously. Don't skimp on the olives.

NONALCOHOLIC MEXICAN MARTINI

Makes 1 drink

1 Combine as for Everyday Mexican Martini above.

4 ounces (120 ml) citrus soda (Sprite, 7 Up, Fresca, Squirt)

1 ounce (30 ml) lime juice

Splash of orange juice

Splash of olive brine

Ice cubes

Green olives

BEERGARITA

Makes 2 drinks

WHY CHOOSE BETWEEN A MARGARITA AND BEER
when you don't have to? Maximize your
intake of toxin-reducing Supplements by
combining both beer and tequila. L'chaim!

1 Combine the ice, tequila, agave nectar,
orange liqueur, and lime juice in a
blender and blend on high speed until
smooth. Pour into two wide-mouth
glasses. Upend (not pour) an open bottle of
beer in each glass, leaving the bottle. Drink
with a straw.

2 cups (93 g) ice cubes

3 ounces (90 ml) tequila

3 ounces (90 ml) agave nectar

2 ounces (60 ml) orange liqueur, such as
Cointreau

2 ounces (60 ml) lime juice

Two 12-ounce (360 ml) bottles Mexican-
style lager

SUPER CLEANSE: We won't tell if you buy frozen
margarita mix. This isn't a fancy drink, after all.

THE MINOR CLEANSE

Makes 1 drink

1.5 ounces (45 ml) tequila
Pinch of cayenne
¼ teaspoon agave nectar
1 lime, quartered

IF YOU ARE FAMILIAR WITH CLEANSING, you might have already tried "The Master Cleanse," also known as the lemonade diet. We've found the positive effects of that cleanse might be lost in the insane hunger you feel while consuming only lemonade for days on end. That's one of the many reasons why the Taco Cleanse encourages multiple hearty tacos throughout the day along with supplemental elixirs. However, we do encourage starting the day with a "minor cleanse" to get your energies flowing. It will activate and open your connection to each of the tacos you will eat throughout the day.

1 Mix the tequila, cayenne, and agave nectar in a small glass. Pour the elixir down your throat, swallow, and suck on a lime wedge.

MIND-LIMBERING MICHELADA

Makes 2 drinks

A PREVIOUS EVENING'S OVERINDULGENCE of Supplements may be apparent upon waking. Use this *cerveza preparada* to postpone these side effects. The michelada is a tomato-based cocktail similar to a Bloody Mary with the same time-manipulation properties. Hand the negative vibrations over to your future self, who may be more capable of dealing with the repercussions.

1 Moisten the rim of 2 chilled glasses and dip the rims into a shallow dish of kosher salt. Pour the beer, tomato juice, lime juice, hot sauce, and Salsa Inglesa into a pitcher. Stir thoroughly. Fill the glasses with ice cubes. Carefully pour the mixture into the pint glasses and garnish with the lime wedges.

Kosher salt for rim

8 ounces (240 ml) chilled lager

One 5.5-ounce (154 ml) can tomato juice

Juice of 1 lime, plus 1 lime wedge for garnish

1 teaspoon hot sauce, such as Cholula

1 teaspoon Spirited Salsa Inglesa (page 116) or vegan Worcestershire sauce, such as Wizard's

Ice cubes

TIP If you are feeling super cleansed, you might want to make your michelada a bit dirty; add a couple of teaspoons of olive brine. If, on the other hand, you are feeling a bit worthless, add a teaspoon of jalapeño brine to ignite your navel center and increase vitality.

LIVING *a* TACO-BASED LIFE

The Taco Cleanse works best if it's incorporated into every aspect of your life. Not only will it help you remember to get your daily recommended allowance of tacos, but it will also make you that much cooler.

Dress up your children as tacos for Halloween. Decorate your house with taco pillows. Buy or sew handsome tortilla warmers. Make a collage of happy people eating tacos and stick it on your fridge. Teach yourself to say taco in every language. A few more suggestions of how you can taco-ize your life are on the following pages.

EXPLAINING THE TACO CLEANSE IN SOCIAL SITUATIONS

By now, you've started your taco journey, and you're already feeling the positive effects in your life. You will surely want to enlighten your friends and family with the knowledge of a taco-based lifestyle. But what happens when your loved ones reject these changes you've made? They might be disbelievers, laugh at you, even try to bully you into eating a burrito. (It's happened, trust us!) What can you do to stay strong in your taco beliefs?

If you're nervous about telling your loved ones about your new cleanse, try this trick from the showbiz industry: Imagine their heads as tacos. It will instantly calm you and put you at ease when having those tough conversations.

You have to understand that your family and friends have seen this before. They've heard about the latest cleanse fad and will probably roll their eyes when you sit them down to tell them. You'll have to put their minds at ease by assuring them that this cleanse is different in every way possible. It's about tacos!

Your coworkers might mock your taco lunch, yet again, and what can you do? First, remain calm. In a controlled manner, repeat back to them what they are saying in your own words—for example, "What you're saying is that you love tacos more than anything, but that eating them as much as possible is a bad thing?" They'll see the irony.

You want your loved ones to adopt a taco-based lifestyle, but they may be resistant. They don't want to change their habits, they worry the diet is too limiting, they just don't understand. You must always keep the lines of communication open, but know that you might have better luck getting a stranger to begin a Taco Cleanse than a family member. Stay strong and taco on. *Namaste*.

RAISING KIDS ON A TACO-BASED DIET

A taco-based diet is appropriate for every age and lifestyle. Children already suffer because they're denied the right to vote, register for their own library cards, or stay up as late as they want. They shouldn't have to suffer a life without tacos.

Life is rough when you're dependent on those around you to meet your needs. So it's up to you to anticipate your baby's and toddler's taco needs. Children under the age of six months will benefit from the positive auras of the taco-eating adults around them, even if they can't quite swallow a tortilla yet. Introduce your children to tacos as soon as they begin solid food. So often young children are deprived of tacos because adults think that youngsters won't like them, while in fact the opposite is likely true. Early findings from our research suggest that perhaps the twos are so terrible because they are sorely lacking in tacos.

School age is perhaps the most important time to feed your children tacos. Tacos have been shown to stimulate the immune system and enhance brain function, both vitally important to children's school performance. We look forward to a time when every day is Taco Tuesday in school cafeterias around the world.

At this time in your children's lives, you still have a great deal of influence over their eating habits. Now is when you'll set your children's culinary habits for the rest of their lives. And heaven forbid they become seduced by the glamorous burrito-eating lifestyle promoted by so many fast-food franchises and celebrities.

They are watching what you eat, so set a good example. Make sure to sit down as a family to eat tacos at least once a week. A few times a year, embark on a Mild or Medium Taco Cleanse as a family. Visit your local tortilla factory or farmers' market so your children can meet the people who make their food. And let your children help prepare the family tacos. Children are much more likely to eat a taco they prepare themselves.

By the time your children are teenagers, you'll no longer be able to shelter them from the influences of the Familiar American Diet. Hopefully, your kids have learned to turn toward tacos to nourish their inner and outer bodies. However, don't be surprised if they go through a rebellious stage and refuse to eat tacos. Cecelia Grant, a longtime taco cleanser, recently wrote to me about her troubles with her son, who insists that taco cleansing is just a faddish money-making scheme preying on gullible consumers who never learned critical thinking skills. What is the world coming to?

If you find yourself confronted with a situation like this, don't force teens to eat tacos with the family. That will only increase their defiance. Make tacos available to them. Be open to honest conversations about how important tacos are for flushing out ultraviolet radicals and cleansing the biological system. Leave this book in a place where your kids can find it, such as under their pillow or in their underwear drawer. In a few years, this stage will pass and your teen will realize you really did know what you were talking about all along. You'll sit down together over a basket of breakfast tacos and laugh and laugh about their foolish anti-taco stage.

MAKING HOLIDAY TACOS

Holidays are a joyous time for celebration with family and friends. But when you're on a Taco Cleanse, things may get a bit stressful. The Taco Cleanse isn't about spending holidays at home on your own; it's about sharing tacos with your family.

Birthdays? You get one every year; why not make it special this time? Last year, Wes had a birthday cake special ordered with fondant tacos on top. Of course, cake isn't a taco, unless it's in a tortilla. Try making a Plantain Tortilla (page 50) and filling it with a slice of cake. Or try the Birthday Cake variation in the recipe for Chocolate-Raspberry Dessert Tacos (page 166). Also, let someone else make the tacos for your party this year; it's your special day!

New Year's Day? Traditional foods for New Year's Day are black-eyed peas, cabbage, and greens . . . all of which are perfect for filling a tortilla. If you're celebrating with friends, bring some Corn Tortillas (page 49) rolled in foil with you, so you can create a Good Luck taco on the go.

Valentine's? If love is in the air, you'll no doubt share some Chocolate-Raspberry Dessert Tacos (page 166) on this traditionally chocolate-centric holiday. If you're single and loving it, then why not treat yourself to a night out at that fancy taco restaurant you've heard so much about?

St. Patrick's? St. Patrick's Day usually falls during spring break, which in Austin usually means South by Southwest, which means lots of crazy music, partying, and green beer. To keep yourself from getting pinched, eat tacos with lots of cooked greens, or keep it raw by making a Collard Tortilla (page 52).

Easter & Passover? Try making an Easter taco by baking sugar cookies and shaping them into taco shells while still warm. Fill with jelly beans and dyed green shredded coconut. Melted Dandies marshmallows will help it all stick together. If you keep kosher for Passover, you're in luck, because tacos work well here. Use the Collard Tortilla (page 52). Add sliced roasted beets, horseradish sauce, and toasted matzo crumbs.

Memorial Day/Independence Day/Labor Day? Summer holidays are traditionally known as excuses to BBQ. There are plenty of ways to have fun in the sun with your friends and eat tacos. The Smoked Brisket and Jalapeño Mac and Cheese Taco (page 149) will likely be the hit of the party. If it's too hot out, try the Tropical Ceviche (page 56) for a refreshing meal.

Halloween? There are taco costumes out there on the Internet, or you can make your own. Don't be afraid to dress as a taco for this spooky holiday. We would not recommend handing out tacos to trick-or-treaters, however. Maybe try handing out good vibes and healing energy to kids who may have never even had a taco.

Thanksgiving? This holiday is easy. The Thankful Sweet Potato Pie Taco (page 162) was made for this day. If you aren't cooking this year or are traveling to visit family far away, bring your own Flour Tortillas (page 47) and simply add your mashed potatoes, stuffing, and cranberry sauce to your taco. Give thanks and rejoice in your taco.

Christmas? A little-known fact is that Santa Claus used to be spelled "Santa Claos," which when you rearrange the letters spells "Nasal Tacos." Legend says he used to inhale tacos before the big ride around the world giving gifts, and that is what empowered him. Whether you choose to believe in Taco Santa or not, give gifts of tacos to your friends and family, and don't be shy giving copies of this book.

Chanukah? The whole point of Chanukah is to eat fried food. What could be easier than putting fried food in a taco? Latke tacos, fritter tacos, fried tofu tacos. If you can fry it, you can fit it in a tortilla.

Q: Why did the young tortilla roll his eyes at his father?

A: Because he was so corny!

TACO YOGA

 Avocado Pit Kneeling on the floor, bring you forehead to the floor. Let your arms and hips release. Connect your heart with the avocado pit as the seed that can create such a magnificent fruit—such a source of richness, flavor, and nutrition. Find that seed inside yourself.

 **Tostada Pose** Lying flat on the floor, stretch your arms up overhead. Spread your fingers and firm the muscles of your arms and legs. Be firm and still, like a tostada awaiting its many toppings.

 Soft Tortilla Lying flat on the floor, allow the arms and legs to be quiet and relaxed. Imagine you are the bottom tortilla in a large stack of tortillas, and let yourself settle down into the floor.

 Upward-Facing Taco Lying on your back, bend your knees and hold your outer ankles. Press the feet into the floor and lift the chest and pelvis. A perfect tortilla provides both the structure to hold many goodies and the suppleness to bend and adjust to the infinite possibility of taco fillings. Likewise, through yoga we aim to achieve a container that is both reliable and supple, so that we may aptly contain our own infinite possibilities.

 Full Taco Pose Lying on your belly, bend your knees and catch your outer ankles. Press the hips in the floor, kick your shins into your hands, and lift the knees and chest. Everyone has experienced the disappointment of a brittle hard-shell taco breaking and spilling precious taco goodies onto their plate . . . or that of a soggy tortilla, unable to support the bounty of goodness, that rips and shreds—again resulting in taco disaster. Thus, through yoga, we seek to become neither brittle nor soggy—but strong and pliable, and ready for all the taco fillings that life has in store for us.

Side Taco Pose From Full Taco Pose, roll enthusiastically onto your right side for a few breaths, then back to the middle, and over to your left side for a few breaths, and then back to the middle. This pose stretches and stimulates the abdominal area, for proper taco digestion. Additionally, this pose works up quite an appetite for more tacos!

Hard Taco Balance on your hips and make your legs and trunk strong and firm—reach the arms out and be a trustworthy container. Keep the mind alert and crisp. Become strong, but not brittle. Stay firm in the pose, as we all know how disappointing a crispy taco shell is when it breaks apart.

Sloppy Taco Pose Lying on your back, bend your knees. Bring your arms out wide, palms up. Let both knees fall to the left for a few breaths, and then to the right for an equal period of time. Your upper back spreads out across the floor like the juicy filling of a taco spreads across the face of a tortilla.

Twisting Breakfast Taco Sitting upright with the legs extended out wide, twist your trunk to face the right leg. Rise and start your day with this pose that brings movement into the spine and gets your tummy ready for tacos. Focus your thoughts on the tacos in your immediate future.

Open-faced Taco Pose Standing, bring the feet wide apart and turn the toes out. Extend your arms out wide and bend the knees. Allow your whole self to open to the glory of tacos. Invite more taco energy into your life and open yourself to receive it.

En Fuego Pose Standing, bring the feet wider than hip-width apart and firm the muscles of the legs. Stretch your arms up overhead and extend the fingers apart. Open your eyes wide and stick out your tongue. You are on fire with the power of tacos! You are the fiery embodiment of taco power!

Inverted Taco Pose With the legs wide apart, extend your trunk forward and down toward the floor. This pose offers a moment to reflect humbly on all that tacos have provided to you in your life. It is a deep bow to Taco-ness.

MY AURA IS WHITE, LIKE A FLOUR TORTILLA.

TACO SALUTATIONS

 exhale

FIRST, STAND TALL. *Gather your hands at your heart as though you are holding a delicious taco. We call this hand position "taco mudra."*

 inhale

RAISE THE ARMS STRAIGHT TO THE SKY *—as though offering your taco potential to the universe.*

exhale

BOWING FORWARD, *bring your taco mudra toward the earth— recognizing that the taco fillings began in the earth as seeds and soil.*

 inhale

RAISE THE HEART *just half way up, extending the heart forward and up —extending the abdominal area.*

exhale

BOW DEEPER *down again, drawing in through the abdominal area (these actions prepare the digestive fire for more taco consumption).*

inhale

INHALE, *sweeping the arms upward and again offering your taco mudra to the heavens.*

exhale

BRING THE HANDS TOGETHER *to the heart, and lower your gaze to the hands in taco mudra.*

TAKE A MOMENT *to connect with all tacos past, present, and as yet unrealized.*

REPEAT *this sacred cycle of taco appreciation.*

TACO MUDRAS

A mudra is a symbolic gesture meant to focus your body's energy—much like a well-made taco.

EXPAND YOUR TACO REACH

Begin with both hands clenched tightly in fists and then stretch your fingers as far and wide apart as possible. Repeat vigorously. This mudra builds your capacity for grasping and containing giant tacos stuffed full with unwieldy and delicious fillings.

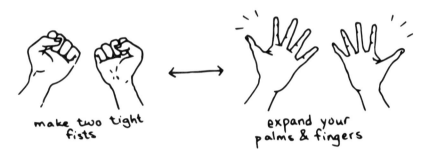

make two tight fists

expand your palms & fingers

MASSIVE TACO MUDRA

Hold both hands, palms up, and cup the hands as though you are holding a large, filled-to-the-brim taco. Allow for space between the fingers. Remember: open fingers, open heart, open mouth.

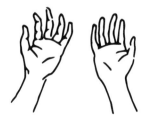

TACO FOCUS MUDRA

Hold both hands palms up, and bringing all four fingers on each hand, firmly cup the hands as though you are holding a taco. This closed finger position develops a laser-like focus for the task of vegan taco consumption.

THE DAINTY WIPE MUDRA

For moments of subtle refinement. Gently swipe the pad of your thumb across your mouth. Tap into the delicate flavors of your taco.

THE FULL TACO CLEARING MUDRA

With your palm facing away from you, wipe the back of your hand clear across your face from one side to the other. This mudra will help you clear away the taco mess on your face and prepare a clean slate for a fresh moment of taco appreciation.

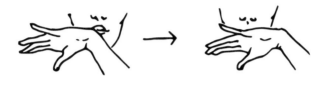

THE PICKY MUDRA

Bringing the tips of the thumb and index fingers together, pinch them tightly. Be sure to keep the pinky up, in order to maintain a quality of delicacy, even as you hone your skills to fuss over the precise positioning of your taco fillings.

PLANTING A TACO GARDEN

Grow a summer Taco Garden in your own backyard. Feel the warm sun on your skin as you cultivate your taco ingredients. After eating tacos with what you grew yourself, you'll never be the same.

Supplies needed:

→ Gardening tools such as a shovel, rake, hoe, gloves

→ Compost and soil to prepare the garden bed

→ Watering can

Seeds or starter plants needed:

→ Corn

→ Tomato

→ Jalapeño

→ Other peppers—serrano, habanero

→ Tomatillo

→ Eggplant

→ Cilantro (likes cooler weather)

→ Red onion

→ Squash (zucchini, yellow, pumpkin)

→ Epazote

Directions:

1 Mix in some compost with your planting soil. Plant your seedlings or seeds in your Taco Garden bed in full sun. The tallest plants (corn) will go in the back so they don't shade the rest. Next will be tomatoes/tomatillos, then jalapeños, onions, and finally cilantro. Water it every day and harvest often!

2 Another taco-friendly method is planting the Three Sisters together. Corn, beans, and squash work together for the betterment of the community. Corn is tall and becomes a pole for the beans to climb. The beans' roots are nitrogen-fixing, which helps next year's crop of corn, and they also help the corn stand up straight in windy areas. The squash shades out weeds and keeps the soil from drying out. After harvest, just mulch all of the remaining vines and leaves in the same spot, and next year's crop will be even better.

OTHER TACO-RELATED PLANTS:

Beans: You could plant beans, and many people have success growing them. They are a long-haul plant, however. You'll need to harvest, clean, and dry the beans for a long time before being able to cook them in a taco recipe. For the amount of space they take up in the garden, and the amount you'll be able to eat, it's generally cheaper and easier to buy them at the store.

Sweet potatoes: These grow in long vines and need plenty of space. Sweet potatoes love the heat, so wait until all sign of frost is long gone. They will grow like crazy all summer, with very little work from you, and then just as it starts getting cool, it's time for harvest. Gently dig out the sweet potatoes! Sweet potato leaves are tasty, too, and can be sautéed like other greens and added to a taco. The potatoes will need to cure for a few days to a couple of weeks, and it can be a bit tricky to set up the right conditions for this, so ask a real gardening professional or utilize the Google for more information. Good luck!

Potatoes: Make a cool potato tower from chicken wire. Layer with hay and potato starts (little chunks of potato with the "eyes"). Put more hay on top. Keep adding hay and some soil when the leaves poke up through about 4 to 6 inches. In the fall, when the leaves turn brown, dig up your potatoes and cure them. They'll need to be cured for about 2 weeks in temperatures between 45º and 60ºF. After that, you can enjoy!

Avocados: WARNING: Warm climates only. Do not read this paragraph if you live in a climate where actual seasons take place. Congratulations! You are the luckiest person alive! You are not only embarking on your taco journey and growing your own Taco Garden, but you live in a part of the world where avocado trees can grow and produce fruit! You might already have one or more avocado trees in your neighborhood. Planting an avocado pit (you've seen it—an avocado pit with toothpicks in a jar of water) is fun and cute, but you won't get actual avocados from it (some never produce fruit; occasionally one will—fifteen years later—but who has time for that?). You'll need multiple grafted avocado trees from a nursery so they have a better chance of cross-pollination. Plant them in a sunny spot where they have ample room to grow; they'll get to twenty feet tall and eight feet wide. When they start to bear fruit, please invite us over to share in your guacamole bounty.

Limes (in warm climates, or in a pot that you bring inside in the winter): Lime trees are less finicky than avocados. Here in Austin, we keep ours outside in pots and bring them inside in the winter, or plant them in the ground and cover them with cozy plant blankets when the temperatures dip below 40ºF. They hate standing water, so plant them with good drainage for the roots. They're pest-resistant, other than to thieving squirrels. If wild animals steal your fruit, just breathe, center yourself, and take pride that the little squirrel will have margaritas for his taco dinner that night.

Mushrooms: Kits can be found at gardening stores, if you are adventurous.

SUCCULENT GARDEN

Supplies:

→ Clean cans and jars from your favorite salsas, chiles, and other taco ingredients

→ Succulents—assorted sizes and shapes

→ Pebbles or polished, colorful glass stones for decoration, optional

→ Potting mix for cacti and succulents

Directions:

Save salsa jars and jalapeño cans that you use during your cleanse, and clean them well. Poke a hole in the bottoms of the cans with a nail for drainage. For the glass jars, put a layer of pebbles or glass stones on the bottom to collect extra water. Fill the containers with cacti potting mix and your choice of succulents. Add extra pebbles to the top of the soil for decoration. The succulents will not need much water or attention, so less is more. We all have a lot to learn from succulents.

COMPOST

Why vegan compost? Compost is the decayed organic material that you can use to fertilize your Taco Garden plants. When you get regular compost from the gardening store, it may contain horse and cow manure, chicken poop and feathers, even ground-up fish guts. Grody to the max. You can buy vegan compost at gardening stores (The Ground Up is a brand found here in Texas), or you can make your own. It's easy, but it takes time. . . .

Start by procuring a compost bin outside somewhere. It could be as easy as a circle of chicken wire on the ground, or as fancy as a $200 tumbler bin from an infomercial. Begin collecting taco food scraps such as broken taco shells, jalapeño stems, tomato vines, etc., and store them in a tightly closed container. If you're lazy, keep them in a zipper plastic baggie in the freezer. If you're motivated, take your taco scraps to your compost bin outside daily. Toss in some dead leaves or grass clippings. Add some dirt if you want. Just try to keep the ratio of "Greens" (your taco food scraps) to "Browns" (dry stuff like leaves) to about 50/50. There are tons of great composting resources out there, such as *The Complete Compost Gardening Guide* by Barbara Pleasant and Deborah Martin, that can help you fine-tune your Taco Compost.

Use #tacocleansegarden to share your pictures!

CROSSWORD

By Matthew Printz

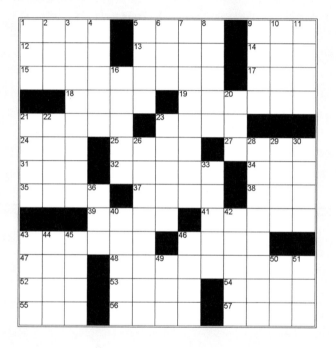

ACROSS

1 Thing to do

5 Access provider, perhaps

9 Ovum

12 Are you _____ the challenge?

13 The cake is _____ (Internet meme)

14 Batman and Robin, e.g.

15 Time to eat some 32-Across

17 Pray and love's partner

18 Guilty, e.g.

19 Another great time to eat a few 32-Across

21 Respectful title

23 Letter opener

24 _____ Jima

25 Prissy one
27 Jared from *My So-Called Life*
31 Wood cutter
32 See 15-, 19-, 43- and 48-Across
34 Horrible review
35 'N_____
37 Rose who belongs in the hall of fame
38 Unwell
39 Faux-cultured
41 Pale and smooth, as skin
43 Excellent time to grab one or two 32-Across

46 *Less Than* _____ (Ellis Novel)
47 Something you might keep in your hole
48 Absolute best time to indulge in eating a couple 32-Across
52 Cartoondom's Szyslak
53 Altar vows
54 Seeks restitution
55 *This Is the* _____ (2012 Seth Rogan film)
56 Small change
57 Greek goddess

DOWN

1 Spot for a soak
2 Spring mo.
3 Peacefully relinquish control
4 Eucalyptus eater
5 Spanish tennis super-star
6 Tofu _____ king
7 Unlawfully obtained
8 Colorful ancient city of Jordan
9 Biblical vegetarian garden
10 Common topping on a 32-Across, abbr.
11 Black-clad listener of Morrissey, probably
16 Neatly groomed or styled
20 Browser destination
21 "_____ Saigon"
22 Game played on the road
23 Risky
26 Industry N.W.A and Ghostface Killah participate in
28 It comes at the end, usually

29 What Dr. Laura does to make a living, these days
30 "For your eyes_____"
33 Spunk
36 When doubled, a dance
40 Indiana Jones's objective, perhaps
42 "Fighting _____"
43 Helen Mirren, notably
44 Madonna was once a pop one
45 What you've got to have
46 Zeal
49 More than you're willing to count
50 That girl there
51 Airport probers

FOR THE ANSWERS, TURN TO PAGE 225!

HELP tHE GUACAMOLE FIND tHE TACO

CERTIFICATE *of* COMPLETIΘN

This certificate is awarded to

in recognition of eating as many tacos as they could for

THE TACO CLEANSE

as certified by **The Institute of Taco Scientists**

Molly R. Kisinger

Jessicaq Morris

Stephanie Bogair

Wes Allison

CUT ALONG THE DASHED LINES AND HANG THIS CERTIFICATE ON YOUR FRIDGE!

LIVING A TACO-BASED LIFE

211

What's Next?

Congratulations, you have completed the Taco Cleanse! Cut out your Certificate of Completion on the previous page or print it out at tacocleanse.com. Frame it and hang it above your desk so everyone knows how amazing you are. Share a photo on social media and tag it with #tacocleanse.

Now it's time to "break the cleanse." You may be really confused about what to eat now. Your body will naturally crave tacos. You may want to start with something easy like a tortilla soup or a taco salad, which have all the comforting flavors of a taco. It will seem strange to imagine cooking something that isn't a taco. Listen to your body-mind. If it's telling you that it's not ready to eat a burrito, then don't force it. You may want to ease into non-taco foods like pizza or falafel, which you can still fold and eat with your head tilted sideways. Maybe try eating these foods for lunch or dinner, while still starting the day with breakfast tacos. Don't try to jump into eating oatmeal or dough-nuts for breakfast right away, unless you wrap them in a tortilla first.

You will have undoubtedly formed a taco community on your journey. Taco friends will stay with you through thick and thin, so make the effort to keep in touch. Occasionally posting taco photos on social media with the #tacocleanse tag lets them know you are still doing well. Reach out to them if you are struggling to decide whether or not to go on another cleanse. Many are taco lifestylists—people who choose to eat tacos for the rest of their lives. A few may even decide to become full-fledged taco scientists. These friends will help you reach your true taco potential. And now that you've finished, you will be able to help new cleansers on their journey. Perhaps you can mentor someone trying tacos for the first time. Maybe you can help a child grow her first Taco Garden. If you live in a place where tacos are hard to come by, consider visiting a taco-friendly city for your next vacation.

Where do you go from here? How will you go on living the rest of your life? You certainly don't want to undo all of your hard work and lower your levels. After a few months of eating non-taco foods, you may wonder if it is time to go on another Taco Cleanse. Don't worry; your body will tell you when it's the right time. Go back to the beginning of this book and read the symptoms in the section titled "Is the Taco Cleanse Right for You?" Even if it's not the right time to taco cleanse again, you can still use these post-cleanse tips to keep your levels high.

→ **Eat tacos a few times a week.**

→ **Continue using Supplements often.**

→ **Go back and reread your taco journal.**

→ **Incorporate clean foods like nachos or taco salads.**

→ **Observe Taco Tuesday.**

→ **Start the day with a Taco Affirmation.**

→ **Practice taco yoga.**

Don't be afraid to live a life away from the Taco Cleanse. Once you've cleansed, you'll always have that experience with you. And another cleanse is only a taco away.

Wishing you health and tacos,

The Taco Scientists

Resources

MORE (AND MORE TRADITIONAL) TACO, TEQUILA, AND LATIN AMERICAN RECIPES

If you're looking for more recipes for tacos or taco fillings or if you're just curious about vegan Latin American cuisine, check out *Vegan Tacos: Authentic and Inspired Recipes for Mexico's Favorite Street Food* by Jason Wyrick and *Viva Vegan! 200 Authentic and Fabulous Recipes for Latin Food Lovers* by Terry Hope Romero.

When we realized that our knowledge of tequila was a bit lacking, we turned to *¡Viva Tequila! Cocktails, Cooking, and Other Agave Adventures* by Lucinda Hutson. Little of that knowledge made it into this book (we're still far from experts), but if you're curious about the varieties of tequila, how it's made, or the culture surrounding it, this book is a gem.

AUSTIN

Our love for Austin permeates this book. Austinite Tips (austinitetips .com) captures much of what we love about the city, as does Chet Garner in his television series The Daytripper. If you're planning a visit, check out Stephanie's guide to the best tacos in town (search "vegan taco guide" at lazysmurf.wordpress.com) and austintexas.org for activities and accommodations.

GOING VEGAN

Eating Animals by Jonathan Safran Foer is a thoughtful introduction to thinking about how animals get on your plate and whether they should. Foer is a fantastic writer and makes the subject accessible and engrossing.

We learned so much about vegan cooking from Isa Chandra Moskowitz and Terry Hope Romero. We recommend all of their books if you're interested in learning how to cook great food without meat, dairy, or eggs, but we recommend *Veganomicon: The Ultimate Vegan Cookbook* as a great general book. *Isa Does It* is a more recent book focused on quick, weeknight cooking.

Eating a healthy vegan diet is pretty easy to do these days, but Jack Norris and Virginia Messina, two registered dietitians, have written a great science-based book outlining what you should pay attention to while crafting your own vegan diet: *Vegan for Life: Everything You Need to Know to Be Healthy and Fit on a Plant-Based Diet*. There is a lot of misinformation on the Internet, so make sure that you are getting any medical information from a licensed expert.

And finally, a great general resource on vegan food, ethics, and lifestyle is vegan.com.

CLEANSING, DIETING, AND BODY IMAGE

It's pretty clear we think cleanses (other than the Taco Cleanse, of course) are unhealthy. For more information about why cleanses don't work and what actually does, check out *Diet Cults: The Surprising Fallacy at the Core of Nutrition Fads and a Guide to Healthy Eating for the Rest of Us* by Matt Fitzgerald.

For a good explanation of why so many of us are stuck on the diet treadmill and how we can get off, read *Health at Every Size: The Surprising Truth about Your Weight* by Linda Bacon.

If you or someone you know is struggling with an eating disorder, please visit nationaleatingdisorders.org.

Acknowledgments

We would like to thank the original contributors to the Taco Cleanse zine, without whom this book would never have happened: Ross Abel, Laura Beck, Kristen Davenport, Mary Helen Leonard, Dinger McPuppenstein, Matthew Printz, Nelly Ramirez, Crystal Tate, Minty Lewis, PS Comics, Jonas Madden-Connor, and Adrienne Lusk. You have true taco spirit!

A huge thank-you to Amey Mathews, certified yoga instructor and creator of the site Vegan Eats and Treats, for creating the Taco Yoga section. We are all standing in En Fuego Pose sending taco power to you!

Thank you to everyone who made special tacos (and taco ingredients) for the cleanse and who continue to make us delicious food: the Vegan Nom, Sweet Ritual, Bouldin Creek Cafe, Capital City Bakery, Cherrywood Coffeehouse, Sue Davis and Counter Culture, the Vegan Yacht, Freebirds World Burrito (they sell tacos, too!), Wheatsville Co-op, Tacodeli, Ctate and Food for Lovers, Gabriel Figueroa and Rabbit Food Grocery, Arlo's Food Truck, Celeste's Best, the Wet Whistle (RIP), Flavour Spot, and Amy's Kitchen.

In addition, the taco scientists would like to thank everyone who enthusiastically cleansed with us and supported the Taco Cleanse from near and far: Andrew and Angela Ramsammy, Joanna Vaught, Chris Rios and Vegan Nom, John McDevitt, Marty the MF Party, Jarvis Black, Isa Chandra Moskowitz, Terry Hope Romero, Sarah Kramer, Chet Garner, Jezebel, Ayinde Howell, Christy Morgan, Lindsay @veganchai, Katie Remis and V Apparel, Caroline Netschert, Nanette

Labastida, Craig Wilkins, Amanda Martinez, Vegan World Radio, the Post Punk Kitchen Forums, Vegan MoFo, Vida Vegan Con, Vegans Rock Austin. With apologies to everyone we're forgetting!

Thank you to Molly Cavanaugh, who found our little zine and saw us through to the end, Matthew Lore, Sarah Smith, Dan O'Connor, and everyone at The Experiment for your work and for making this book possible at all.

And of course, our families: Ken and Julie Gezella, Mike and Barb Morris, Jenna Morris, Megan Rigos. Matthew Printz, who watched the Taquito while I wrote and tested recipes, and all the Printzes and Frisingers for believing in me. Thanks to John, Mary, Chris, and Michael Allison for letting me be myself, again. Thanks to Dan Bruce for trying every taco I ever made, no matter how ridiculous. Sandra Benson for coming to Austin to help with food styling and introducing John Stamos to the Taco Cleanse. Amanda Schmoker for making some pottery in the book and all your support. Radmila Bogdanich and George Bogdanich for being really excited for the Taco Cleanse even though they didn't always completely understand it. And Lana Bogdanich and Alex Basich for being the cutest pair of phish tacos ever.

Everyone who bought a copy of the zine, everyone who used the hashtag #tacocleanse.

And finally, Austin, for making us fall in love with tacos.

Index

NOTE: Page references in italics refer to photos of *recipes*.

Crossword Solution

About the Authors

WES ALLISON was raised in the Gulf Coast confluence of Southern, Tex-Mex, and Cajun cuisines. After transitioning to a vegan diet, he was naturally drawn to re-creating the comfort foods of his youth. He began his stint in the food service industry after moving to Austin, Texas, in 2009. He continues to get a kick out of cooking unconventionally for friends and for the Maximum Salad YouTube channel.

STEPHANIE BOGDANICH grew up in Springfield and Chicago, Illinois, where she spent her childhood watching *Star Trek*, learning the name of every dog she met, and insisting her Serbian grandmother prepare her tacos. She moved to Olympia, Washington, in 1998 to pursue her education at the the Evergreen State College, where she studied taco science, among other things. In 2003, she moved to Austin, Texas, where she discovered the astonishing variety of tacos and spent the next eleven years in search of the perfect taco.

MOLLY FRISINGER was raised on the traditional Jewish-Texan diet of migas tacos and bagels. She realized her calling as a taco scientist when she left the warm embrace of Texas for the cold, tacoless chill of Philadelphia for college. Good tortillas were nowhere to be found and the only salsa was THAT salsa. You know. Upon returning to Texas, Molly vowed she'd never be tacoless again.

JESSICA MORRIS grew up in the crunchy taco shell region of East Texas. After college, she moved to New York City and dreamed of the breakfast tacos of her homeland. After she came to her senses, in 2008 she moved to Austin in pursuit of better tacos and the dream of opening the first all-vegan grocery store in Texas, Rabbit Food Grocery. She now devotes her life to taco science and vegan junk food.